T0313028

ROUTLEDGE LIBRARY EDITIONS: INDUSTRIAL RELATIONS

Volume 32

THE PRICE OF TUC LEADERSHIP

THE PRICE OF TUC LEADERSHIP

BRYN ROBERTS

LONDON AND NEW YORK

First published in 1961 by George Allen & Unwin Ltd

This edition first published in 2025
by Routledge
4 Park Square, Milton Park, Abingdon, Oxon OX14 4RN

and by Routledge
605 Third Avenue, New York, NY 10158

Routledge is an imprint of the Taylor & Francis Group, an informa business

© 1961 George Allen & Unwin Ltd.

British Library Cataloguing in Publication Data
A catalogue record for this book is available from the British Library

ISBN: 978-1-032-81770-5 (Set)
ISBN: 978-1-032-80094-3 (Volume 32) (hbk)
ISBN: 978-1-032-80130-8 (Volume 32) (pbk)
ISBN: 978-1-003-49552-9 (Volume 32) (ebk)

DOI: 10.4324/9781003495529

Publisher's Note
The publisher has gone to great lengths to ensure the quality of this reprint but points out that some imperfections in the original copies may be apparent.

Disclaimer
The publisher has made every effort to trace copyright holders and would welcome correspondence from those they have been unable to trace.

BRYN ROBERTS

THE PRICE OF
TUC
LEADERSHIP

LONDON

GEORGE ALLEN & UNWIN LTD

RUSKIN HOUSE MUSEUM STREET

FIRST PUBLISHED IN 1961

© *George Allen & Unwin Ltd.*, 1961

PRINTED IN GREAT BRITAIN
in 11 pt. Juliana type
BY THE BLACKFRIARS PRESS
LEICESTER

ACKNOWLEDGMENTS

This book would never have been completed without the valuable help of my dear wife, Vi, and Miss Hamby, my very efficient secretary.

While Vi devoted herself to extracting and checking references from TUC Reports and other documents and, as is to be expected from one of her kindly nature, frequently exhorting me to soften my justifiable criticism of the TUC, Miss Hamby not only did the entire typing and indexing but also proved invaluable in obtaining verification of facts and dates and assisting me in the general work of research.

I am deeply grateful to them both.

July 28, 1960

White Cottage
Scotts Lane
Shortlands
Kent

CONTENTS

INTRODUCTION

In this book I register severe criticism of the TUC General Council; indeed, I charge that body with the responsibility for Labour's defeat in the 1959 General Election, as well as the decline in the influence and effectiveness of the trade union movement.

But, it may be said, why should I criticize the General Council when for twenty-seven consecutive years—1934 to 1960—I have sought election to that body?

Will it not be said that I am squeezing sour grapes and venting my spleen for having been rejected, year by year, by millions of block votes, and that these criticisms are but the outpourings of a disappointed man unable to see things objectively?

Acknowledging these possible reactions, allow me to say that the views expressed in this book are neither the result of a sudden revelation nor an outburst of personal anger, but are consistent with what I have said, on behalf of my Union, at Congress after Congress over many years.

It is true that I have established a record, not likely to be surpassed, in the number of times I have been unsuccessful in the annual ballot for the General Council. However, it is also true that I could have become a member of the Council without submitting myself to the ballot, as admission by a side door was offered me.

In 1941 the late Lord Dukeston (then Mr Charles Dukes), General Secretary of the National Union of General and Municipal Workers, invited me to his office to have a chat. When we met we were each accompanied by a colleague [Capt M. Hewitson (NUG & MW) and Mr Arthur Moyle (NUPE)], both of whom are now Members of Parliament.

After a friendly conversation I was asked to consider leaving my NUPE post and taking up a very lucrative appointment with the NUG & MW.

It would have provided me with a substantial salary increase (about three times what I was then receiving), a safe seat in

Parliament plus the salary that went with it (the sitting Member was seriously ill and not expected to live), together with a seat on the TUC General Council, plus other payments for contributing to the NUG & MW's Journal and addressing meetings in various parts of the country. Other prospects were outlined, and upon acceptance our respective solicitors were to be brought in to draw up an appropriate legal agreement with these terms in mind.

While I appreciated the generous offer of Lord Dukeston and the high motives that prompted him to make it, I advised him that the principles of trade union organization which I was endeavouring to promote in NUPE were irreconcilable with those upon which the general type of union was based, and that I could not, without disregarding deeply held convictions, accept his very generous offer; I therefore declined it. Later, during the 1941 Edinburgh Congress, the NUG & MW General Secretary repeated his offer, and although I again rejected it because I believe the general type of union is out of joint with the times, it did not affect our friendly relations, which continued until his death in 1948.

Trade unions are the product of an industrial environment, brought into being to perform specific purposes. When the environment changes the trade unions are inevitably affected, and unless they adapt themselves to such changes they lose their effectiveness and are compelled to pursue activities quite contrary to their original aims and ideals.

One hundred and twenty-six years ago Robert Owen, a great reformer and trade union leader, brought into being the Grand National Consolidated Union. It was a great triumph and expanded rapidly, frightening the employers and the Whig Government in the process.

Members of the Grand National thought at the time that they had found the answer to all their industrial troubles, and that by making their Grand National stronger they would be assured of protection and fair treatment from their harsh employers.

But this mammoth organization, with its rather impractical aims, did not endure. The industrial scene was rapidly changing. In spite of lofty and inspiring slogans and appeals for workers' unity, the Grand National, failing to meet the needs of the time, passed into decline and eventually disappeared.

The demise of the Grand National did not halt the development of other types of trade unions; it increased that development. The less spectacular but more realistic craft and general unions, in spite of legal difficulties and other obstacles, plodded slowly but steadily on as the workers' protectors. For over a century they rendered magnificent service to their members and families.

Many of these craft unions have published accounts of their formation and development, together with a record of sacrifices endured and reforms achieved. They are rich, moving and unforgettable chronicles of earlier days of the trade union movement.

But the conditions prevailing a hundred and more years ago are vastly different today. From the handicraft phase to the factory system that followed it, we have passed to the age of modern production, accompanied by technological and electronic aids.

As the Grand National Consolidated failed to meet the needs of the industrial environment in the 1830s, the craft unions that succeeded it (and likewise the general type of union that began to develop in the 'nineties) are now, in a similar way, failing to meet the industrial requirements of the 1960s.

The bench has largely given way to the conveyor belt. The shovel has been replaced by the excavator, and the productive system hitherto dependent upon the hand and eye of skilled craftsmen is now giving way to automatic processes and mass production.

Both the craft and the general union forms of organization, instead of reflecting industrial needs, are now in conflict with them, and, try as hard as they may, it is impossible for them to ensure their survival and also fulfil their original trade union purpose.

Until this is acknowledged and the craft, general and other unions adapt themselves to present-day requirements and remove all forms of competitive trade unionism, with its accompanying disorder, there is little likelihood of any real progress being made towards the establishment of a socialist Britain.

The disorder that arises from the present outmoded and competitive trade union structure accounts for the ever growing conflict and confusion that now affect both the trade union and the political movement, and, whatever the right or the left may say, it is this trade union disorder, and not Mr Gaitskell or Mr Jay, that has made Clause 4 of Labour's constitution meaningless and its retention or revision of no consequence. The extension of public ownership and the establishment of a planned economy are utterly impossible while a chaotic, unplanned trade union structure prevails.

The purpose of the trade union movement is to bring about a transformed society, yet by its failure to adapt itself to the times and revise its century-old habits it is taking on the appearance of a rabble.

Conflict with employers takes second place to conflict between Union and Union. Without consultation or agreement one Union will take a certain course of action that may, and frequently does, throw thousands of members of other Unions idle.

Actions of this sort are bringing all Unions into public disrepute and is causing many trade unionists themselves to lose confidence in their own movement.

And while the influence and effectiveness of this great movement declines and drifts from its original principles, the TUC General Council, which represents the leadership, has been content to look on.

It has dismally failed to give guidance to the millions of members it claims to lead, and it must bear the responsibility for the tragic situation in which the movement now finds itself.

The fact that there are dozens of competing Unions in every major industry (excepting coal mining) destroys all hope of any real extension of social ownership, and it compels the Labour Party to adopt substitutes such as 'investment in industry', etc., which are alien to the faith and purpose of the Labour movement. This shows the price that has to be paid for the failure of TUC leadership to keep its own house in order.

It is said that the TUC leadership has no power to intervene in the affairs of the affiliated Unions. That's a shocking excuse, because every time it has been proposed that such power should be bestowed upon the TUC leadership it is the leadership that has objected to accepting it.

The fact is, as the record shows, that the TUC leadership has no desire to take an active role in general trade union affairs. It prefers to remain 'above the battle' when Unions are fighting the employers or when Unions are fighting one another. Members of the leadership may be earnest and well-meaning men, but, apart from one or two, they regard the present TUC set-up as sacrosanct and for many years they have fiercely resisted every proposal to alter it.

Although I believe that trade union reconstruction will never come about on the initiative of the undemocratically elected TUC leaders, whose desire to perpetuate the present anachronistic TUC machine transcends all other considerations, other forces will surely arise to achieve it.

There is no fundamental conflict between the members of craft unions, general unions and industrial unions. They all have a common interest, and if this is pointed out and explained to them (and this the TUC leadership has dismally failed to do) they will readily respond to the call to re-model their Unions on modern lines.

When it was explained to the members of my own Union that it would be preferable to have one representative Union, instead of several competing Unions, to speak and act for local government employees, they readily agreed that NUPE should take steps to establish this.

Accordingly, at a conference convened by the TUC, and with the approval of our National Conference, NUPE proposed that

every Union operating within local government, i.e. General and Municipal Workers' Union, Transport and General Workers' Union, Confederation of Health Service Employees, Fire Brigades' Union and the National Union of Public Employees, should pool all their local government members, and from such pooled membership an entirely new organization, bearing a title different from any of the Unions involved, should be created.

That every trade union officer, including the clerical staffs, now acting on behalf of the separate Unions, would be absorbed in the new representative single Local Government Union, with all existing salaries, conditions, superannuation, etc. fully protected; the chief offices to be filled in accordance with a procedure to be determined by all the interests involved in the pool.

Here was an opportunity to remove trade union disorder from the local government sphere. Although NUPE is proud of its title and its history and has accumulated substantial reserves, its members readily agreed to the proposed merger. But the members of the other Unions never had the opportunity to accept or reject the proposal—they were never consulted.

It is not surprising that inter-union conflict is more intense today than it has ever been.

But I still retain my faith in this great trade union movement, despite the fact that it is now so badly directed.

As a pit boy in a Welsh coal mine at the age of thirteen I became a trade unionist and a member of the Labour Party, and have remained so ever since.

That the movement, notwithstanding the present divisions and disorder, will eventually achieve its historic mission I have no doubt.

CHAPTER 1

TUC: A MINORITY MOVEMENT

In Britain there was at October 1959 an estimated working population of 24,190,000, most of whom are eligible to be members of trade unions affiliated to the TUC.

Unfortunately, the TUC has so far only commanded the allegiance of just over one-third of this working population.

In the war and post-war years from 1939 to 1957 a steady increase in TUC membership to a maximum figure of 8,337,325 was recorded, but when the membership figures for the year 1958 were reported they revealed that a membership recession had set in and that over 160,000 had been lost.

It appears from information available that this loss is not likely to be a temporary one, and it is feared that when the figures for 1959, 1960 and later years are published they might well reveal an even greater membership decline.

But even if this dismal prophecy does not materialize and the TUC succeeds in maintaining its present membership strength, it will still be a minority movement having less workers inside its fold than there will be outside.

The TUC leadership seems to have no ambition to alter the present balance between the organized and the unorganized sections of the industrial community.

Although under Rule II of the TUC Standing Orders the leadership is authorized 'to assist in the complete organization of all workers eligible for membership of its affiliated organizations', it is quite impossible, on account of conflicting trade union interests, for the leadership to do anything worthwhile to achieve this.

It would be easy to arrange national recruiting campaigns and for the President, General Secretary and other TUC leaders to address meetings in the various industrial centres. But such meetings would produce more casualties than recruits unless the leaders of all other Unions were allowed on the platform to say their piece and also ensure that the TUC orators didn't say anything to the special advantage of their own Unions and the disadvantage of others.

In the shipbuilding centres Mr Ted Hill, leader of the boilermakers, would no doubt be the TUC spokesman for 'complete organization'. If asked, would he be able to advise a non-unionist in the shipbuilding industry which Union he should join without causing a riot? Would he be able to iron out such demarcation problems as to who should 'twang the string' or bore the holes?

And how fascinating it would be to attend a TUC recruiting meeting convened under Rule II in a railway centre, addressed by Messrs Webber (TSSA), Hallworth (ASLE & F) and Greene (NUR), either in their capacity as leaders of their respective Unions or as leaders of the TUC! It might be rather too much, anyway, to expect that these three members of the TUC General Council would agree to share a common platform, but if they did, what a row there would be!

And what would ensue if Sir Thomas Williamson, of the General and Municipal Workers, and Mr Frank Cousins, of the Transport and General Workers, together with Mr W. J. Carron, of the Engineers, visited such industrial centres as Birmingham, Manchester or Glasgow, in accordance with their obligations as members of the TUC General Council, and addressed mass meetings in these centres in order to *assist in the complete organization of all workers eligible for membership of affiliated Unions*?

These three eloquent TUC leaders would undoubtedly attract many non-unionists to their meetings, and they have the ability to state an effective case demonstrating the advantages of being a trade unionist.

But the fun would commence if the non-unionists present were to ask the advice of the three TUC spokesmen as to which of the 186 affiliated Unions they should join.

Would Sir Thomas, in a spirit of generosity, advise the 'nons' not to enrol in his own general Union but to join the general Union led by Mr Frank Cousins, and would Frank Cousins counter this noble and sacrificial act by advising them to sign up with Sir Thomas?

And what guidance would Mr W. J. Carron offer the 'nons'? Would the spirit of generosity displayed by Sir Thomas and Mr

Frank Cousins also affect him? Would he read to the mass meeting the names of the thirty-nine Unions inside the Shipbuilding and Engineering Confederation, together with the names of the Unions outside the Confederation, and advise the 'nons' to join any of them except his own AEU?

What a beautiful story that would be if it came true! But that is unlikely. The TUC leaders are too wise to expose to mass view the present chaotic trade union structure they seem so anxious to preserve.

Rule II, providing for '*the complete organization of all workers eligible for membership of affiliated Unions*', will therefore continue to adorn the Standing Orders of the TUC, but, like Clause 4 of the Standing Orders of the Labour Party, it will be for appearances only.

What recruiting campaigns there may be will be left to subordinate TUC officers to organize through this or that Trades Council, because although this produces trivial results it keeps up the pretence that the trade union movement is a united one.

Moreover, to increase trade union membership on the required scale in order to end its present minority status would need extensive preparation; it would be necessary to re-model the Unions on modern lines; it would involve the elimination of inter-union conflict and the scrapping of the fraudulent 'Bridlington rules', making it possible by a re-alignment of union boundaries for Unions to co-operate together for the realization of common objects, instead of being bogged down, as they now are, by selfish and sectional aims.

Such a membership drive would also require the establishment of well-manned enrolment centres throughout the country where new members could be properly assigned, not to any old Union, but to the one catering for the industry in which they work; it would also call for an enormous quantity of leaflets, booklets and posters, etc. describing a new, imaginative and inspiring trade union programme for the entire movement, as well as the intelligent use of the large numbers of trade union organizers who now, instead of increasing overall trade union membership, fight each other in order to retain for their respective competing Unions their share of the diminishing trade union pool.

A planned, well-directed campaign on these or similar lines

would undoubtedly produce a rich membership harvest and invigorate the trade union movement.

Unfortunately it is unlikely to appeal to the well meaning but mentally rutted leaders of the TUC. The invasion of a mass of new members would not only bring about extensive quantitative changes, but far reaching qualitative changes would also follow that might be most disagreeable to the present smug and complacent leadership.

It would most probably endanger the present balance of power between the General Unions, Craft Unions, Industrial Unions and others.

Such an invasion of new members which a campaign of this sort would bring would also affect the present allocation of seats on the TUC General Council, and it might make redundant those leaders who now represent minorities and bring in leaders who are not only more representative but whose outlook is also more in keeping with the times.

Alas! under present TUC leadership such an expansion plan would have no chance whatsoever.

The movement may continue to languish and its power and influence go on declining; Labour may lose the next three General Elections as it lost the last three, but all this is unlikely to have any effect upon the attitude of the present leadership.

While members of this leadership represent conflicting interests generated by competitive types of trade unions, they always succeed in subordinating any differences that might arise between them, in the interests of their own security.

Over many years they have, with skill and subtlety, designed a pseudo-democratic constitution and established a remarkable set of rules which enable them to quell any internal opposition that might appear.

Discordant in private, united in public, these elements representing the leadership have not only learned how to live together; they have also succeeded, within the General Council, in reconciling the irreconcilable.

CHAPTER 2

TUC: ITS PUBLIC RELATIONS

When Bill Grundy of ITV, in the programme 'Searchlight', visited Oxford to cover the contest between Prime Minister Macmillan and Sir Oliver Franks for the Chancellorship, he endeavoured to reveal to the viewers what the people of this University City were thinking. Questioning one undergraduate he enquired who was the General Secretary of the TUC. The reply he received was that the holder of the post was Mr Frank Foulkes!

Although this reply may be gratifying to Mr Frank Foulkes and somewhat disconcerting to Sir Vincent Tewson, the undergraduate need not feel too bad about giving Bill Grundy the wrong answer because hundreds of thousands of trade unionists themselves are no better informed.

This is no reflection on Sir Vincent, but it does help to show how pathetically inadequate are the TUC public relations.

The Trades Union Congress has existed since 1868. One hundred and eighty-six trade unions are affiliated to it; in 1959 it had an annual income of £325,000 and it represents 8,176,252 members. Its Central, or General, Council consists of thirty-five members selected in a most peculiar way (as we shall show in a later chapter), and of these thirty-five members twenty-five are trade union General Secretaries and the rest are either trade union Presidents or National Officers or District Secretaries, all of whom hold important full-time posts in their respective Unions.

The General Council is served by an administrative staff numbering eighty, and these are appointed by the General Secretary.

The General Council itself meets regularly each month. From the members of the Council numerous committees are constituted, such as Finance and General Purposes; Economic; Education; Organization; International; Production; Social Insurance and Industrial Welfare; and Disputes; on which Committees the members of the General Council are expected to serve.

Members of the General Council also sit on numerous Joint Committees, Consultative Committees, Advisory Committees, Special Inquiries and many other bodies. They have frequent meetings with the Government itself and make constant representations to the various Ministries.

Time and attention must also be devoted to the National Council of Labour, upon which the Labour Party and the Co-operative Movement are represented.

Frequent conferences at home and abroad have also to be attended.

Some of the more prominent members of the General Council also have paid part-time jobs on the nationalized Boards and Public Corporations, and not a few undertake other onerous duties not covered by the long list we have given.

One member of the General Council who also leads a Union of nearly 1,000,000 was reported in *Target*, the Bulletin of the British Productivity Council (January 1960), to have travelled in 1959 no less than 30,000 miles in connection with his duties for his own Union and as Director of the Industrial Training Council; Chairman of the Confederation of Shipbuilding and Engineering Unions; member of the National Production Advisory Council for Industry; member of the Machine Tools Advisory Council; member of the Engineering Advisory Council and also of the National Joint Advisory Council and of the United Kingdom Council of the European Movement; President (British section) of the International Metalworkers' Federation; Council member of the Air League of the British Empire; Deputy-Chairman of the British Productivity Council; and also as an associate with several educational establishments.

No one can deny that the members of the General Council, who constitute the TUC leadership, live most arduous lives, and it is regrettable that on account of their hopeless public relations only they themselves are able to appreciate the sacrifices they have to make.

To one who only has the duties of a General Secretary to carry out and finds that looking after some 200,000 members is about as much as he can manage, it is truly amazing that the TUC

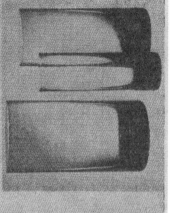

LABOUR

The TUC Magazine

June 1960

SIXPENCE

Industrial News *FOR THE USE OF THE PRESS*

ISSUED BY THE TRADES UNION CONGRESS

CONGRESS HOUSE, GREAT RUSSELL STREET, LONDON WC1
GENERAL SECRETARY: SIR VINCENT TEWSON CBE MC
PRESS AND PUBLICATIONS OFFICER: C.H. HARTWELL
TELEPHONE: MUSEUM 4030

No.7.

April 8, 1960

CONTENTS OF THIS ISSUE:

PRO AND CON OF P.B.R.

Some of the piece-work schemes used in industry almost defied understanding by the trade unionists whose job it was to negotiate around them, when claimed by them as hard-won rights - chairman of the T.U.C. Production Committee when opening a two-day discussion conference on payment by Results at Congress House recently.

The advance of automation meant that industry would probably see less of payment by results systems in the future, Mr Wright told his audience of closely trade unionists. But, he added, a great number of P.B.R. schemes were currently in operation and it was the purpose of the conference, organised by a T.U.C. and attended by members of 40 of its affiliated unions for a two-day range of interested to examine these schemes and to explore their merits and defects.

The complexity of many P.B.R. schemes was also dealt with by Miss Sylvia Shimmin, one of four specialist speakers at the conference.

Miss Shimmin, an industrial psychologist currently engaged in industrial research, said the systems of P.B.R. which were simple and easy to understand were now few and far between. As a consequence, workers frequently misunderstood the relation between their work performance and the cash they received in their pay packets.

Theoretically, said Miss Shimmin, P.B.R. schemes assumed that the work done was determined by the worker's response to the money incentive. But, she said, the relationship was not a simple one and depended on the links on home earnings, often because the belief of a worker's control over his output and his earnings. Attempts to vary and overcome these externally imposed limits could affect the quality of work, warned Miss Shimmin.

...the workers' side, said Mr Chandler, understanding and co-operation could best be obtained by allowing workers to take part in the work study investigation. A workers' representative, trained in work study methods, should become a member of the work study team.

leaders should be able to find the time and the energy to carry out properly all the requirements expected of them.

It's a great achievement if they can! To be able to read the daily newspapers, journals, Government documents, reports of Parliamentary proceedings and other essential publications; to find time to give thought to economic and political developments and devote attention to current strikes and internal strife; look after the interests of the members of their own Unions and shape the industrial lives of 8,176,252 TUC members, could only be performed by supermen, and it is regrettable that we are not able to identify who these remarkable men are!

It is true that at Congress House there are over a dozen different departments managed by trained permanent staff, but it would be unkind to suggest that this permanent staff not only shapes the policies of the leadership but also advises the leadership how to carry out such policies.

This uncharitable thought is discarded because one of these departments, known as the 'Press and Editorial Department', does its job so inadequately that even an Oxford undergraduate is led to believe that Mr Frank Foulkes, and not Sir Vincent Tewson, is the General Secretary of the TUC!

This perhaps is unfair to the TUC Press and Editorial Department, because this department may be the greatest victim of the present trade union disorder and may be prevented by TUC leaders from pursuing any enlightened policy that may cure such disorder.

In this age of radio, television and mass propaganda it baffles understanding that TUC relations with the public and its own 8,176,252 members should depend upon a little twenty-page magazine called *Labour*.

This magazine, apart from the annual Congress Report, is the only organ the TUC leadership regularly circulates.

It is a dreary publication, which has a circulation of only 14,000. It is never seen on the bookstalls. It is never advertised and its editor never invites contributions, and only non-controversial items are ever printed in it.

In the railway industry, for instance, the three Unions (NUR, TSSA and ASLE & F) are frequently in conflict with each other, and their differences are from time to time reported in the public press in a manner that does much damage to the trade union movement.

It would be instructive and might help to soften or remove the conflict between these three Unions if they were to state a case in the official TUC organ for their different viewpoints, particularly as each of the leaders of these three Unions is also a member of the TUC leadership!

But that would never do. For the TUC to reveal and discuss inter-union grievances before the membership would be like parents discussing private matters before the children.

It might increase the circulation of the TUC magazine and stimulate the members to take action to remove the causes of the conflict, but to do that by showing that some affiliated Unions washed their clothes brighter and whiter than other affiliated Unions would, in the eyes of the TUC leaders, be most undesirable.

Relatively few shop stewards or branch officials know of the existence of this official TUC publication, which is apparent when it is shown that if the monthly issue of 14,000 copies were to be divided amongst the 8,176,252 affiliated members it would provide less than two copies for every 1,000 members, and if the 14,000 copies were equally divided amongst the 186 Unions attached to the TUC each would have but seventy-five copies.

While the TUC leadership itself could hardly claim that this twenty-page magazine with such a small circulation throws much light on the industrial scene, or reveals to the 8,176,252 brethren and the general public what the leadership is thinking and doing, it is, of course, supplemented by the free distribution of a stencilled document known as *Industrial News*.

After each of its monthly meetings the General Council issues *Industrial News*, which consists of three foolscap pages of type matter reproduced on a duplicating machine. It contains the decisions reached by the General Council and is handed to the representatives of the press for their information, and two or three copies of this duplicated statement are also sent to each affiliated Union.

If, in this three-page 'hand-out', the press boys find a newsy item, such as a reference to the affairs of the ETU, the 8,176,252 trade union members will be able to read varied and imaginative interpretations of it in the newspapers the following day.

Usually, these duplicated sheets deal with very humdrum affairs containing no spicy bits for the press to exploit. In these circumstances the press completely ignores the 'hand-out' and then neither trade unionists nor the public has the slightest idea what the TUC leaders are doing or in what direction they are going.

But, after all, we should be grateful to the press boys because, while they may ignore some of the best items in the 'hand-out' and give the wrong slant to others, they are the only public relations officers the TUC possess!

In public relations the spoken word can be as powerful as, if not more powerful than, the written word. Perhaps the TUC leaders are inclined to attach more importance to the spoken word? They are good orators and they have wonderful opportunities to use the spoken word by meeting trade unionists in great mass meetings in all parts of the country and utilizing radio and television to explain and justify TUC aims relating to public ownership and to deal with other problems of the day.

By meeting trade union members in this way the members would be able to know who their TUC leaders are and appreciate what they are attempting to do. It would enable the TUC leaders to explain the harm that unofficial strikes inflict not upon the employers but upon the workers themselves (which would be far more effective than holding secret inquiries about them), as well as show the need for trade unionists to co-operate in promoting orderly industrial development in order to secure a steady rise in their living standards; they could also command public approbation by using their eloquence to end inter-union struggles and demonstrate the need for a reform of trade union structure.

But the leaders shun these opportunities. They have even less regard for the spoken word than they have for the written word.

In a democracy one of the most vital requirements of leadership, if it intends to survive and flourish, is to keep its own supporters, as well as the public, informed about its activities, and by the skilful use of both the written and the spoken word to win new adherents and counter any hostile criticism immediately it appears.

But to expect the TUC leadership to carry out these elementary and essential functions of leadership is just wishful thinking. They won't do it because the present crazy TUC set-up prevents them from doing it, and if they attempted it they would be exposing themselves to public ridicule and imperilling their own position.

In a venture of this sort it would be necessary for the TUC leadership to have a common policy, and this it will never be able to devise while its General Council of thirty-five members, twenty-five of whom are General Secretaries, represent conflicting interests and competing organizations.

If mass meetings were to be organized and radio and television talks arranged, this collection of leaders could not agree on what should be said unless it was a string of meaningless generalities. In this incredible TUC outfit darkness is preferred to light.

In the absence of a common policy no one is trusted to speak for the leadership—not even the TUC President.

This has been acknowledged again and again. It was clearly revealed by Mr Bob Willis, who presided over the Blackpool Congress in September 1959. He made a first-class speech, but he was compelled to say:

I understand the President's speech is his own speech; it reflects neither the point of view of an organization nor of the General Council. (1959 Congress Report, page 85.)

Whatever Mr Willis said, therefore, had not the slightest effect upon the proceedings of Congress. While some may have cursed or praised him for what he said, no one must question him about it nor must his speech be discussed, and after the usual vote of thanks for delivering it the matter is ended.

His speech is just an interlude, like, say, a soloist in any annual rally.

In the hope of improving the TUC's public relations and to make the TUC rank and file more acquainted with what was being done in their name, the National Union of Public Employees thought it advisable to try to induce the TUC to publish a weekly journal, and at the 1944 Congress NUPE tabled the following motion:

Recognising the increasing range of the activities of the Trades Union Congress and the important position it occupies in the life of the nation, this Congress believes that the publication of a weekly journal by Congress is essential.

This Congress believes that through the medium of such a publication the activities of the Trades Union Congress would be made more widely known and its work better appraised; it would provide the means to expound the social and industrial programmes of the Trades Union Congress and to counteract the propaganda of those who may oppose such programmes; it would enable trade union membership to be more effectively fostered; it would present opportunities to promote a better understanding of national and international problems, and changes in the structure of trade unions, necessitated by changing circumstances, could also be encouraged. Such a publication would be an invaluable instrument in serving the needs and aspirations of the workers.

Therefore, this Congress requests the General Council to take immediate steps to launch an informative and attractive weekly journal designed to command popular support, and to appoint competent editorial and other staff that may be necessary to ensure this. (1944 Congress Report, page 308.)

In support of this motion NUPE argued that the activities of Congress had become too important to be dealt with by occasional press hand-outs or by issuing scrappy monthly bulletins; that the need for continuity in our publicity was evident and that without it this great movement was as Samson without his hair.

Early in the debate the then Sir Walter Citrine, who was TUC Secretary, intervened to say that 'with the sentiments of the motion the General Council would be in accord . . . but the better way to approach this problem would be for the General Council to look carefully into it and see whether they could devise something which was likely to be a success and not a drain upon the funds of Congress'. After it had been said that the publication of a TUC weekly journal 'would not be fair to the Daily Herald', the motion was referred to the General Council for consideration. That was sixteen years ago, but TUC publicity and its public relations today remain as they were then, in 1944!

It is true that the Daily Herald has had connections with the Labour movement since 1911. In 1929 the TUC acquired forty-nine per cent of the shares in the Daily Herald (1929) Ltd. and became joint owners with Odhams Press Ltd. This entitled the TUC leadership to be represented on the Daily Herald Board. The late Ernest Bevin did great work in fostering the Herald, but when he and a few others left the scene and their places were taken by lesser men, and as competitive union and personal interests became more acute, such pressure was put on the Herald editorial staff by the TUC leaders to do this and not to do that

that it became almost perilous for them to make any comment on our political or industrial affairs. The only really free hand the staff had was in the presentation of racing tips and gardening notes!

Under this censorious and unimaginative policy the *Daily Herald* declined to such an extent that Odhams Press Ltd. advised the TUC leadership of its intention to withdraw from the 1929 joint arrangements. In 1957 a new agreement was forced on the TUC which enabled the *Daily Herald* staff to exercise complete editorial freedom. Since this 1957 agreement the *Daily Herald* has been a far better paper although it is now under the complete control of a capitalist firm!

As the TUC leadership has hardly convinced us that it can run a daily newspaper successfully, would it, if it acquired one, run a weekly journal any better? It is very doubtful.

Since the 1944 Congress at Blackpool, when NUPE proposed that the TUC should publish a weekly journal, which proposal was referred to the General Council for its consideration, the TUC leaders have not shown any enthusiasm for it.

It seems, however, that they did not wish to ignore Congress completely because four years later, in January 1948, the General Council decided, no doubt as a sort of substitute for a weekly journal, to publish each week a two-page trade union supplement in the right wing *Forward*, edited by Mr Francis Williams. Mr Williams was delighted at this decision of the TUC leadership, which he described as *'an important development in the history of trade union journalism'*.

This two-page supplement carried the title 'News of the TUC and its Allied Unions'.

But it proved a frost. No one was authorized to give *Forward* any 'news of the TUC', and no informative articles or announcements from the pens of the TUC leaders appeared.

Only by scrounging round journals already published could the editor find material to fill the two pages and this stuff had nothing to do with TUC affairs.

When *Forward* died a peaceful death on March 25, 1960, the two-page supplement 'News of the TUC' had shrunk to but four half-columns. It is not known whether the demise of *Forward* was due to the printing of this remarkable supplement!

In the light of this failure to produce a mere two-page supplement, it is unlikely that the TUC will embark on anything more ambitious.

In any case, a TUC weekly journal would require the services of an exceptionally clever editor. Indeed, it is doubtful that there is a person yet born able to interpret the views and the policies of a collection of leaders most of whom are bent on travelling in opposite directions or in no direction at all.

In such circumstances the least said and written about TUC affairs the better—that is the form of 'public relations' which the TUC leadership prefers.

CHAPTER 3

TUC: ITS RELATIONS WITH CONGRESS

The 'ABC of the TUC', a sixpenny pamphlet published by the TUC, explains that:

Congress invariably meets on the first Monday of September and remains in session for the following four days. It is presided over by the General Council member who has acted as Chairman of the Council since the preceding Congress. As soon as Congress is over, the Chairman (if re-elected to the Council) becomes Vice-Chairman and the General Council elect a new Chairman who, twelve months later, will preside at Congress.

Affiliated Unions are entitled to send to Congress one delegate for every 5,000 members or part thereof. Delegates must, at the time of their appointment, be working at their trade or be permanent paid officials of their union.

The first paragraph calls for no comment, apart from expressing a doubt as to whether the necessary continuity and efficient control of a movement more than 8,000,000 strong can be served by the General Council appointing a different Chairman every year on grounds of length of service.

This 'ABC' pamphlet then goes on to say that 'the Congress has three main functions:

(1) It considers the report of the work done by the General Council during the previous year; . . . '

The General Council certainly submits a voluminous report to the delegates attending Congress. But this report is largely history. It reveals what the leadership has done, but it is most coy in respect of its future intentions.

The TUC salaried staff exercise great care in its presentation, and if any one of the 186 affiliated Unions objects to any particular part of it its representative can, if he disregards the obvious impatience of the delegates anxious to get on with the hundreds of items on the agenda, exercise his right of protest by moving the 'reference back' of the paragraph to which objection is taken, in a speech limited to five minutes.

It is a very rare thing for a 'reference back' to succeed. The subject raised and the reply from the platform may be of little interest to the other delegates, and this disinterestedness is certainly an asset to the leadership when the vote on the 'reference back' is taken.

The prospect of changing policy on any vital issue, either within the General Council or within Congress itself, is remote. The machinery of the TUC has been devised to prevent it.

The second main function of Congress, as described in the 'ABC' pamphlet, is:

(2) Congress discusses and takes decisions on motions forwarded for the agenda by affiliated Unions.

To the 1959 Congress the affiliated Unions submitted 76 motions, and of these 18 were composited. Following debate 26 motions were carried, 9 were defeated and 9 were referred, by agreement, to the General Council for consideration.

Congress certainly 'discusses and takes decisions' but that's about all it can do and about as much as the leadership wishes it to do, because, as the 'ABC' pamphlet acknowledges, *'neither Congress nor the General Council can override the autonomy of the affiliated unions'* and *'none of their decisions is binding upon the affiliated unions'*.

In fact, Congress is more like an annual meeting of a debating society than a deliberate assembly. This suits the leadership excellently, because if Congress adopts any motion which the leadership dislikes it can, with constitutional justification, disregard such motion.

One year Congress may carry by an overwhelming majority a motion dealing with a most important issue of policy. This successful motion is then passed to the leadership, who, in turn, will pass it to a committee, and representatives of the Union or Unions promoting the resolution will be invited to attend the Committee, but apart from a short, vague paragraph or two in the subsequent General Council's report nothing more is likely to be heard about it. The next year, however, Congress may reaffirm this motion, but beyond recording the reaffirmation in the record of Congress the leadership is unlikely to take any further action. In the following years the motion may be repeated or expressed in slightly different terms, and each time it is presented to Congress it may again be carried by big majorities. Congress can discuss and reach decisions on motions; it can also reaffirm them and repeat and revise them, but one thing it cannot do: it cannot compel an unwilling leadership to carry these decisions out.

It seems incredible that serious-minded men and women, year after year, devote their time and energies to get Congress to adopt motions which, under the present TUC set-up, can never be implemented.

Although the TUC leadership does not carry out the decisions reached by Congress (unless they are minor and very general decisions), and pleads that it hasn't the powers to do so, it goes to great lengths to ensure that Congress shall not reach decisions which the leadership does not favour.

Each year the affiliated Unions may feel strongly on some subject or other. It might be wage restraint, or automation, or joint consultation, or redundancy, or the forty-hour week. On these and other important subjects resolutions may be sent in in batches by several Unions; some of the resolutions will be loosely worded or of a pious character, while others may demand positive action and be more troublesome to the leadership.

In these circumstances the technique of 'grouping' comes into operation. This is a remarkable device. Ostensibly, it is designed to facilitate Congress business by reducing the number of motions on the agenda by compositing them when there is more than one on the same subject.

In this event, the Unions promoting the motions are requested to attend the Grouping Committee on the Saturday prior to the Congress opening on the following Monday. A selected member of the TUC General Council will preside over the Committee and he will endeavour to reach agreement on the terms of a single composite motion to take the place of several separate motions. This invariably means that the Unions are pressed to sacrifice parts of their original motions as a prerequisite to securing agreement for the suggested composite.

There is usually much argument, but in due course a roughly drafted composite begins to take shape. A minority of the Unions represented on the Grouping Committee may dissent from the

C

terms of the suggested composite for many and varied reasons. It may be argued that if they (the minority) accept such a composite the most vital part of their own motion would be destroyed, or if they subscribed to the terms of the suggested composite they would be committing themselves to support something to which their Union is completely opposed.

Usually, by this time the presiding General Council leader will have passed the crisis. He may not have secured unanimous agreement for the suggested composite but, except for the minority who refuse to be associated with it, he has the majority lined up. He then invites the majority to select the mover, seconder and those who wish to speak in support of the composite.

Invariably the terms of the composite motion agreed to by the majority of Unions attending the Grouping Committee are agreeable to the TUC leadership. It will have priority and a friendly reception.

The minority—it may be only one Union—is likely to be called before the Standing Orders Committee and pressed many times 'to be reasonable and agree to the composite'. Despite the fact that the minority regards the majority composite as negative and completely unsatisfactory it is sometimes subdued and gives in, but on occasion it sticks to its guns and insists upon exercising its right by demanding that its original motion shall be submitted to Congress.

It needs some courage to do this. Congress itself will be made aware of the attitude of the minority, and as the majority composite will be taken first the speakers supporting it, more often than not, instead of stating a case for their own composite, prefer to devote much of their time to attacking, to the satisfaction of the leadership, the promoters of the minority view.

No matter how good the minority case may be, the majority composite, which is invariably pious and woolly and makes no specific demands on the leadership, is certain to be a winner when the vote is taken.

The minority composite or the single union motion, which expresses itself in specific terms and calls upon the leadership to take certain positive action, is pretty certain to be heavily defeated.

While the wordy battle proceeds the TUC leaders occupy their seats on the platform with an air of apparent detachment. Not all the thirty-five constituting the General Council elect to sit on the platform. Quite a number, particularly those members of the leadership who are General Secretaries, prefer to sit in the body of the hall with their delegates. This gives them the opportunity to catch the President's eye, enabling them to intervene at any time, especially when the platform is hard-pressed. When called, instead of speaking from the platform as members of the leadership, they are able to use the delegates' rostrum and give the delegates the impression that they are speaking for their delegations.

First appearance would suggest that members of the leadership who prefer to take their seats on the floor of Congress instead of taking their proper places on the platform are in conflict with their General Council colleagues. But that is not so. It is good strategy for the leaders to divide themselves up on the platform and on the floor of Congress, and by their good co-operation and the big card votes they hold they are invariably on the winning side.

But so crazy is the present TUC set-up that even after spending hours of argument within the 'grouping' committee, and later spending time and energies in the ensuing debate, it would not have made the slightest difference if the minority composite had been carried instead of the woolly, pious majority one.

If the minority composite had been carried nothing could have been done about it because the leadership would contend that it had not the power even to attempt its implementation; and as the woolly, pious composite doesn't ask the leadership to do anything in particular we are, in any case, back where we were.

On occasion, however, things don't go according to plan and sometimes the leadership is decisively defeated by Congress. But such a defeat only inconveniences the leadership, because it can't be compelled to change its policy or adopt a new one. It simply acknowledges its defeat and then takes steps to evade the consequences of it.

A notable defeat for the leadership took place at the Margate Congress in 1952, when a composite motion of a most positive character was carried by 4,542,000 votes to 3,210,000.

The terms of this motion, which the leadership opposed, called upon Congress to reaffirm the faith of Congress in the principles of social ownership; denounce the intention of the Tory Government to denationalize the steel and road haulage industries; call upon the General Council to formulate proposals for the extension of social ownership to other industries and services, particularly those subject to monopoly control.

What happened to this motion which the 1952 Congress carried by such a decisive vote will be described in subsequent chapters, and it will be shown that whether the leadership wins, loses or draws it can, under the present TUC set-up, by manoeuvre and manipulation, thwart the will of Congress and prevent the entire movement from proceeding in the direction it wants to go.

Having dealt at some length with what the 'ABC of the TUC' pamphlet describes as the second important function of Congress —'to discuss and take decisions on motions forwarded for the agenda by the affiliated unions'—let us refer to the third main function which the pamphlet lists. It is that

Congress elects by ballot vote the General Council (or the leadership) for the coming year.

This statement is as inaccurate as it is brief. How is it possible for Congress to elect by ballot vote a General Council of thirty-five persons when twenty-four of this number have been given reserved seats before Congress meets and before the delegates have even seen the so-called ballot paper? Besides, the vast majority of the delegates will not have the slightest idea who are the contestants for the unreserved seats, and would only be able to identify the more colourful occupants of the reserved seats.

In fact, Congress does not elect the General Council. It accepts the list, which is a good old totalitarian practice.

It is rather regrettable that the leadership circulates the 'ABC of the TUC' as an educational pamphlet! It is not only misleading to say that Congress elects the General Council by ballot vote, but the very basis on which this so-called ballot rests is a phoney one which lends itself to the 'bartering of votes', about which charges are made in Congress from time to time.

This is not due to the culpability of the leadership but reflects the prevailing trade union disorder, which grows ever more acute.

The composition and election of the General Council rests on eighteen trade groups, plus one group for women workers, and each group is allocated an imaginary number of unions and an imaginary number of members.

Here is the statistical statement showing (1) the trade groups, (2) the number of unions and (3) the number of members, which was published in the 1959 TUC Report.

	Trade Groups	*No. of Unions*	*No. of Members*
1	Mining and Quarrying	5	716,927
2	Railways	3	508,200
3	Transport (other than Railways)	11	1,347,584
4	Shipbuilding	5	130,726
5	Engineering, Founding and Vehicle Building	27	1,517,113
6	Iron and Steel and Minor Metal Trades	16	208,699
7	Building, Woodworking and Furnishing	18	542,222
8	Printing and Paper	13	326,766
9	Cotton	6	134,030
10	Textiles (other than Cotton)	23	94,084
11	Clothing	7	163,848
12	Leather and Boot and Shoe	5	101,144
13	Glass, Pottery, Chemicals, Food, Drink, Tobacco, Brushmaking and Distribution	15	470,689
14	Agriculture	1	135,000
15	Public Employees	4	277,498
16	Civil Servants	8	465,583
17	Non-Manual Workers	15	255,028
18	General Workers	4	781,111

This statement gives a completely false picture. It is all guess-work because not even the TUC Research Department has the slightest idea as to the number of Unions or trade union members there are in these eighteen Trade Groups, yet it is on this that the ballot is based!

Let's take a couple of samples to show this. Railways (Group 2) are credited with three Unions and 508,200 members, yet actually there are forty-two Unions representing many thousand additional workers in the railway industry.

Take another example: Group 14—Agriculture. The TUC statistical statement shows that there is only one Union (the

Agricultural Workers' Union), with a membership of but 135,000 in this Group. This also gives a completely false picture because the Transport and General Workers' Union and several other Unions also represent agricultural workers.

Take Group 18—General Workers. The entire membership of the National Union of General and Municipal Workers is credited in this Group, yet this same Union has, in fact, members in the industries and trades falling within every one of the eighteen Groups.

No comment is offered on the Women—Group 19, because this Group is so remarkable that no Unions or membership are listed at all. What it represents is anybody's guess.

At the 1950 Brighton Congress the National Union of Public Employees sought to end the publication of this incorrect 'statistical statement' by moving that:

Any affiliated organization having members covered by more than one Trade Group shall report to the General Council the number of members it represents in each Trade Group, and this information shall be presented in the statistical statement in the Annual Report. (1950 Congress Report, pages 535-537.)

NUPE pleaded that it was vital that correct information should be in the possession of the General Council; that it should know how and where our trade union membership is spread, where our weakness is and where our strength lies; that it was desirable to submit truthful, reliable statistical data and not a lot of figures that had no relation to the facts.

Immediately after the motion had been moved and seconded the spokesman for the leadership rose and advised Congress to turn it down. He contended that it would be difficult to collect and submit statistics of the kind suggested by the motion; that it would be undesirable to reveal the precise disposition of trade union members; that it would place a tremendous task on the affiliated Unions.

The advice of the leadership was accepted by Congress and the motion which sought to publish truthful, and not false, statistical information was rejected.

For the leadership to acknowledge that it was too difficult to collect accurate information concerning its own membership and deliberately advise Congress to agree to the continued circulation of statistical information which is palpably untrue, not only indicates the chaotic state of trade union organization but also shows the decadence of the leadership which countenances this chaos.

It is ten years since this was raised at the Brighton Congress in 1950, and the leadership continues, each year, to issue these false statistical membership statements.

It seems inconceivable that leaders who are for ever advocating a planned and more efficient industrial system acknowledge that they cannot exercise control of their own members, and are, in effect, compelled to publish these 'cooked' figures.

At one point of our history our opponents claimed that 'Labour was not fit to govern'. This indictment would certainly not be out of place if it were made in respect of the leadership of the TUC.

The relationship of the TUC leadership to Congress is a peculiar one. In theory Congress is the superior body, but in practice it is subordinate. This is due partly to the fact that members of the leadership are able to play dual roles. What they fail to accomplish as members of the General Council they succeed in accomplishing as leaders of their respective affiliated Unions. The present disorderly trade union structure, which enables them to play this sort of game, suits them fine, and they have no desire to change it.

CHAPTER 4

TUC: ITS RELATIONS WITH THE MEMBERSHIP

Except for the recluses and the mentally sick, almost everybody knows and can identify the present Tory Prime Minister and his chief Ministers and is aware of their policies, vague though they may be.

But how many of the 8,176,252 trade union members can name and identify the present TUC President and its General Secretary, and how many are aware of the policies of the TUC, vague though these may be?

In various parts of the country, amongst various groups of rank and file industrial workers, including public employees, we conducted a sort of 'Gallup poll' in the hope of collecting information that would give us some idea of what trade unionists were thinking and their knowledge of TUC personalities and policies.

To both questions the 'don't knows' were in a majority. To the question 'Who are the present TUC President and General Secretary?' we certainly collected a mixed bag, which included the names of dead leaders and retired ones, but for the post of President most of those quizzed thought that the present holder was Alan Birch, with Will Lawther in second place. For the post of TUC General Secretary Sir Vincent Tewson headed the list, Sir Tom O'Brien being not far behind.

To the question 'What are the TUC's policies?' most of the replies, other than the 'don't knows', were rather rude ones and we refrain from quoting them, but some of the replies showed that those quizzed believed the TUC 'wanted wages kept down' and 'wanted the workers to produce more'.

We do not attach undue importance to this little quiz. It was nevertheless extremely depressing to note the many erroneous, absurd and hostile comments made about the TUC, and we hope that they are not typical of the attitude of the millions of non-active, card-carrying members.

If this were the case the future of the trade union movement would be bleak indeed and the blame for it would lie with the TUC leadership for its failure to establish any effective contact with the membership.

The leadership might deserve criticism for some of the things it does and for many of the things it fails to do, yet it cannot be denied that, assisted by a staff of eighty, it has many things to its credit. But by isolating itself from the workers and by being so inarticulate, the leadership, even when it brings about certain improvements, gets little credit for it because the overwhelming majority of the workers has no means of knowing how these improvements were brought about or how they were achieved.

The improvements are taken for granted, like the sun and the rain.

As industrial affairs become more complex, and as more and more Joint Councils, Joint Committees, Federations and Confederations are formed to soften the conflict between numerous competing Unions, here again the successes achieved by trade unionism are not always apparent to trade union members.

As negotiations in respect of wages, hours and working conditions are, in the main, conducted through these joint bodies, over which the single Executives have little control, the result is that the authority of the Union Executive, which is the keystone of sound trade unionism, is being gradually undermined.

The Union Executive becomes subordinate to these joint bodies. It is pushed farther away from the industrial scene, prevented from having direct contact with its members, and it becomes increasingly dependent on the shop stewards. As this development proceeds trade unionism weakens and indiscipline grows.

There is no effective remedy to this truly alarming state of affairs while there are numerous competing and conflicting Unions operating in the same industry, although the evils arising from this senseless competition could be minimized if the TUC leadership acted responsibly and played its part and did its duty in guiding and inspiring the working community, which now drifts along like a rudderless ship.

But it is apparent that the TUC leadership has no intention of taking steps either to remove competing trade unionism or to do anything worthwhile to mitigate its evils, except to print and circulate a couple of hundred booklets making quite unrealistic appeals for 'greater trade union unity', which, in effect, means the preservation of the present disorderly and chaotic set-up.

Whatever influence the TUC leadership had on the mass of trade union members, that influence is undoubtedly declining, although nothing is being done or is likely to be done to alter this disastrous trend. These complacent TUC leaders have the power as well as countless opportunities to play an effective part in our industrial affairs, but it seems that they do not wish to disturb their quiet, uneventful lives.

The failure of the leadership to take advantage of Rule 23 of its own Standing Orders is but one instance of this. The rule states:

the General Council shall, subject to the approval of the (Congress) General Purposes Committee, be permitted to submit an emergency motion for the consideration of the delegates to Congress.

This rule gives the TUC leadership the opportunity to present to Congress for its endorsement any policy it desires to counter or advance in relation to industrial affairs, trade union organization, international activities and other subjects, in order to guide the trade union movement as an effective leadership should.

Unfortunately, the TUC General Council does not construe it to be its duty to exercise such leadership. For it to table a motion of its own, under Rule 23, might not only cause it to become involved in troublesome questions, but might also reveal internal conflicts within the General Council, which, by ignoring Rule 23, now remain hidden.

This rule could be an instrument of enormous importance, yet the leadership has dismally failed to make effective use of it. It could be used to draw attention to the urgent need for trade union reconstruction and highlight this problem as an issue of supreme importance, requiring the attention not only of Congress but of the entire trade union membership.

This emergency instrument could also be used by the leadership to enlighten and instruct, as well as to marshal opposition against the objectionable and unwise decisions of the Tory Government, including its provocative action in abolishing the

Industrial Disputes Tribunal. It could have enabled the leadership, with the authority of Congress behind it, to express the entire trade union movement's condemnation of the Government's action in imposing the veto on a properly negotiated wage settlement involving Health Service staffs.

By availing itself of Rule 23 the leadership could have drawn attention to the coal crisis, the plight of the redundant miners and the benefit that would accrue from a national fuel policy, which private enterprise is incapable of applying.

It would also have given the leadership the opportunity to associate itself with other ill-treated sections, such as the shockingly underpaid railwaymen and farm workers, and make authoritative statements with the full backing of Congress on their behalf.

These are but a few of the domestic issues that could have been publicized in emergency resolutions which an uninhibited leadership could have tabled on the annual Congress agenda to the advantage of the entire movement.

Other subjects, including international events, which have so frequently shocked our moral standards and seriously damaged general trade union principles, could also have been dealt with under this rule, to the undoubted enhancement of the influence and reputation of the TUC.

By the bold and intelligent use of Rule 23 alone the TUC leadership could not only have created in the minds of trade union members the right mood to ensure a Labour victory in the 1959 General Election, but could also have commanded the gratitude of the workers in the industries that have been helpless victims of the so-called 'free play of the market' under private enterprise.

What lessons could have been taught and what advantages gained if this Rule 23 had been intelligently used!

But the TUC leadership doesn't wish to draft resolutions and publicize to the 8,000,000 or so members statements that may incite discussion or compel it to take sides on public issues.

They don't wish to disturb, much less arouse, the workers from the deadly apathy which now afflicts them. The leadership prefers them to remain quiescent.

Let's give credit to the leadership for selling 14,000 copies of its monthly magazine among 8,176,252 trade union members! Apart from this, what does the leadership convey to the millions in the wide open spaces of industry about the problems of the day?

Does it take its members into its confidence and explain to them the TUC's policy, say, on wages? Does it explain what it proposes to do to bring about a shorter working week? Surely the TUC has something to tell them about what it is doing or proposing to do in respect of redundancy and contracting industries, that constitute a real nightmare to the workers?

Trade unionists would also welcome some indication of what the leadership proposes to do to ensure that they will enjoy their due share of the prosperity accruing from technological development and be able to participate in effective joint consultation and play a real part in management.

What a different atmosphere there would be amongst the workers if the leadership, instead of remaining so shy, provided a little enlightenment on these subjects. But it studiously avoids doing this.

Members of the leadership, on infrequent occasions in Congress, may make vague and inconclusive 'lead in' speeches on some of these various subjects, but these speeches, together with any resolutions of the affiliated Unions that may be carried, are then quietly buried in the official report and quickly forgotten, as the record shows—and the workers in factory and workshop will know little, if anything, about it.

That's the traditional TUC routine!

As we cannot deal here with all these vital questions let us take but two of them: wages and hours.

It will be generally conceded that in Britain, where distances are relatively short and ethnological and climatic conditions so similar, without any radical differences of social or political control, we should have a wages system reflective of these conditions. Surprisingly enough, our wage structure, if it can be so called, is responsible for the most anomalous and inequitable state of affairs. As these anomalies and inequalities become more acute, the victims, many of whom are stalwart trade union members of long standing, come to believe that the leadership is either indifferent to these evils or is incapable of taking any action to remove them. Whatever the reason may be, many of these victims lose faith in trade unionism and sever their connection with it.

But it is neither indifference nor incapacity that accounts for the leadership doing nothing to iron out these anomalies. The leadership believes, as its pronouncements show, that the present system, with all its defects, is the superior one and that it would be disastrous if a national wage policy were to replace it.

Although the leadership has avoided enlightening the millions of wage earners as to its reasons for clinging to the present wage system and for believing that an untried national wage policy would prove disastrous, it is not our purpose here to argue the merits or the demerits of such a policy, because, whether it is superior or not, it is quite impossible to introduce a national wage policy while we have such trade union chaos, with dozens of different Unions operating in the same industry.

Perhaps the leadership realizes this. Ten years ago, in 1950, the leadership—the General Council—appointed a special committee to consider the wages issue. The committee included Lincoln Evans (now Sir Lincoln), A. Deakin, W. Lawther (now Sir William), J. Tanner, T. Williamson (now Sir Thomas) and Charles Geddes (now Sir Charles).

The committee seems to have devoted much time to this important matter, and in short neat paragraphs it published in the 1951 Report its views on the effects of rearmament, the balance of payment problems, price reduction, profits control, the question of wages and finally 'the attitude of the TUC leadership'.

In paragraph 382 (page 283 TUC Report 1951) the committee recorded this remarkable conclusion:

It is apparent that in the present situation trade unions must endeavour to maintain the real wages of their members by demanding wage increases. Some favourably placed sections may be able to achieve this, but it is not likely to be possible for workers as a whole.

The claim that the trade union movement exists to serve and protect the workers was shattered to smithereens by this amazing TUC decision.

In effect it amounted to an act of abject surrender by the leadership. Instead of marshalling trade union forces intelligently and responsibly, and striving to secure a fair deal for workers generally, it divided them into the 'favoured' and the 'unfavoured', to the evident delight and satisfaction of the leaders of private enterprise, who took full advantage of it.

This 'devil take the hindmost' attitude of the TUC leadership, which amounted to a confession that it was helpless to shape or even influence the course of wage movements, could hardly be regarded as a clarion call to the unorganized workers to become trade unionists !

Nearly ten years later, in 1959, the TUC leadership made a very similar confession in respect of the claim for the forty-hour week, as is indicated on page 287 of its report to the 1959 Blackpool Congress, which states:

The 1958 Congress remitted to the General Council (the leadership) a motion asking them to call a special conference of unions interested in the forty-hour week in order to arrive at a unified policy. When the General Council considered the motion in November they reiterated their belief that the way in which the forty-hour week was to be achieved was primarily a matter for individual unions, and they took the view that a TUC campaign might well be an embarrassment to the unions . . .

This extract from the General Council's 1959 Report shows that the attitude of the leadership towards the forty-hour week claim is very similar to the conclusions set out in its 1950 Report on wages. While in 1950 the leadership could do nothing other than divide up the members into 'favoured' and 'unfavoured' sections, in 1959, as the above extract from its report shows, it pleaded that if a TUC campaign for a forty-hour week claim were to be conducted by the leadership it *'might well be an embarrassment to the unions'*, and it could not approve that a unified policy, under the direction of the General Council, should be pursued but that the forty-hour week claim should be left to each of the 186 affiliated Unions to pursue as best it could.

Under this guerrilla directive of the leadership the merit of a forty-hour week, which is the admitted aim of Congress, is completely disregarded. The strong, well-positioned affiliated Unions may be able to win it, while the weak ones will not.

In principle, the decision of the leadership on wages in 1950 is similar to its decision on hours in 1959. Both decisions are the negation of trade unionism. Instead of the favoured helping the unfavoured and the strong helping the weak, the TUC leadership is content to look on while trade unionists become the helpless victims of the free play of private enterprise, which it makes no attempt to restrain or control.

The plea that the General Council, on behalf of all the 186 affiliated Unions, should endeavour to bring about in an orderly fashion the introduction of a forty-hour week, by opening immediate negotiations with the employers' national organizations and the Government, was made in vain at the 1959 Blackpool Congress. The leadership has no wish to be involved in questions of wages, hours and other matters of direct importance to the 8,176,252 members. It prefers to remain aloof and detached from these mundane affairs. It has no relations with the workers in the wide open spaces of industry because it has no desire to establish such relations.

CHAPTER 5

ARCHITECTS OF DEFEAT

Harold Hutchinson, a well-informed journalist, writing in the *Daily Herald* on October 19, 1959, estimated that in the October 1959 General Election '3,000,000 trade unionists either voted Tory or did not vote at all'.

Even if Hutchinson were to be a million out in his calculations, it would still present a grave indictment of those responsible for trade union leadership over the past decade.

This trade union leadership, having dammed and diverted the trade union stream, no longer serves a progressive purpose. It has long ceased to inspire the young trade unionists and has created widespread cynicism in the minds of many of the older ones.

Brickbats should not be flung at Douglas Jay for declaring that there should be *'no further nationalization'* because that has been the real intention of the TUC leadership since long before Labour's defeat on October 8, 1959.

Jay's remarks should not divert attention from the occupants of Congress House, who were the real architects of this defeat.

By their acts of omission and commission they discredited public ownership; they made nationalization a dirty word; they lamentably failed to exercise any influence over industrial struggles except to sit back and wait for attrition to force a settlement of these struggles; and by abandoning the inherently peaceful purposes of the trade union movement in national and international affairs they caused many trade unionists and other members of the public to believe that world peace would be more secure in Tory hands than it would be in theirs.

They ensured Labour's third consecutive electoral disaster.

These leaders are motivated by prejudice. They issue from their 'Ivory Tower' their pronunciamentos denigrating and affronting both persons and nations whose ideals and sense of values happen to differ from theirs. Recklessly they burn their boats behind them and lead the acquiescing trade union move-

48

ment to the point of no return, leaving the cleverer and more enterprising Tories to take full advantage of their erring judgment.

At home the leadership offers no alternative to the principles of private enterprise, while abroad, instead of cultivating working class understanding and endeavouring to allay national conflicts, it seems to delight in aggravating ideological differences.

It has no peaceful role. It led in the campaign for German rearmament, which rearmament is now acknowledged to be the greatest danger to world peace.

It has opposed disarmament. At the 1958 TUC at Bournemouth (pages 398-402, 1958 Congress Report) it was moved by NUPE that

This Congress recognizes that the present level of military expenditure, amounting to over £1,500 millions, is largely responsible for the present inflationary situation, as well as the curtailment of essential capital investment, the indefinite postponement of the required highway construction and the freezing of plans for new hospitals, schools and slum clearance schemes.

Congress also recognizes that the present excessive military expenditure is also responsible for the drastic cuts in the social services, and makes it increasingly difficult to preserve or improve wage standards.

Further, Congress recognizes that the present strained industrial atmosphere and the intransigent attitude of the Government and employers to reasonable wage claims are to a great extent attributable to the burden of armament costs, which can only be borne by imposing greater hardship on wage-earners and their families.

While our national and world interests should be defended, Congress believes that our present scale of military expenditure, instead of increasing our security, is undermining our economic foundations and exposing the nation to great peril.

This Congress cannot subscribe to the present enormous burden of arms—of weapons before wages—and it calls upon the General Council to have discussions with the National Labour Party without delay, for the purpose of considering the formulation of a programme providing for the drastic curtailment of military expenditure.

The General Council put up one of its most able leaders, Sir Alfred Roberts, to advise Congress to reject this resolution. In the course of his speech he declared that

Any drastic reduction in the programme for defence would have a considerable impact on employment. I mention it and leave it at that.

D

Continuing, Sir Alfred went on to say:

The General Council are prepared to have a look at this, not in the terms of the motion, but with regard to seeing that money for defence is properly spent and not wasted . . . I am authorized by the General Council to ask Congress to remit it so that we can have a look at it. If that is not acceptable I must say that the General Council will oppose the motion.

The motion was opposed and on a card vote it was rejected. However, if, as the TUC spokesman said, it was TUC policy to see that money for defence was 'properly spent and not wasted', its vigilance doesn't seem to have been very effective, because, apart from other shocking examples of flagrant waste, Chapman Pincher, in the *Daily Express* of April 7, 1960, declared that 'more than 660 millions, mulcted from the taxpayers since the war, had been spent by the Government on missiles which have either flopped or failed to arrive before they were obsolete'.

As the present military expenditure is acknowledged even by the TUC leadership to be a great burden to the nation, and particularly to the workers, it is not unreasonable to expect that the leadership should do everything possible to establish peaceful co-existence in order that the burden can be made lighter, but unfortunately it regards every attempt on the part of Soviet Russia to bring about peaceful co-existence as an evil Communist ruse.

A few affiliated Unions, to their credit, have endeavoured to increase East-West trade. But they commanded little support from the leadership, in spite of our vulnerable economic position, until Mr Macmillan visited Moscow, negotiated an Anglo-Soviet trade agreement and laid the foundation of a Summit Conference.

Prime Minister Macmillan, with his white Russian hat, could claim with some justification that friendly relations with Soviet Russia, trade and peace were safer in his hands than in the hands of his political opponents.

The TUC's attitude towards the Soviet Union has been as intolerant as it has been unimaginative. It even provoked Mr Kruschev, the most Liberal-minded leader ever to rise in Russia, to declare publicly that if he lived in England he would vote Tory.

The TUC's attitude towards China has been even more reckless. In 1958 the Chinese Federation of Trade Unions, representing over thirty million members, invited the TUC to send a delegation to China. The TUC abruptly rejected the invitation on the grounds that the trade unions in China 'are not free'. It thus slammed the door on a nation of over 600,000,000 whose future industrial and communist activities may be most important to Britain and the world.

Until the formation of the present Mao Tse-tung Government China was largely a nation of illiterates. For this illiterate industrial army to throw up overnight, without Government help, trade union leaders and branch officials able to speak, write, keep accounts, advise, negotiate and administer the newly created national Unions, covering a country larger than Europe, was clearly impossible, and for the TUC leaders to snub this movement of over thirty million strong and declare it to be 'not free' because the Chinese Government and social reformers assisted the movement, shows how prejudice and ignorance guide the decisions of the present TUC leadership.

The Tories did not win the 1959 General Election; the TUC leadership presented it to them.

The Tories were able to pose as the Party most likely to secure peace, disarmament, co-existence and the continuity of industrial prosperity.

Is it surprising that 3,000,000 trade unionists believed them and took their side?

It would be unwise to assume that this desertion of 3,000,000 trade unionists from Labour's cause during the course of a General Election is but a temporary setback that can be rectified in time for the next contest. The consequences of TUC leadership are likely to prove more permanent than that because this mass political desertion betokens something more serious than a mere switch of voters from one Party to another. It reveals the declining faith in Labour's cause and shows that the bonds that formerly knitted the wage earners together have become loosened and in many cases completely shattered.

In earlier days, to belong to the working class was a popular and proud claim. Increasing numbers now regard it as a stamp of inferiority, while trade union unity and solidarity, which millions suffered untold sacrifices to preserve, have less and less significance.

TUC leadership cannot evade its responsibility for this decline in the spirit of trade unionism. Indeed, in many ways it has encouraged this decline.

For many years this leadership has been drifting towards moral bankruptcy, and the high ideals and the great values that brought the trade union movement into being are disappearing and the philosophy of 'I'm all right, Jack' is rapidly taking their place.

The early post-war years were years of great promise and led countless trade unionists to believe that the New Jerusalem was almost in reach, but it proved to be but a mirage.

The taking over by the 1945 Labour Government of mines, railways, electricity, gas and airways was to be the beginning of a great economic transformation, but due to the failure of the trade unions to adjust themselves to meet the needs of these nationalized industries they have developed into bureaucratic monopolies in which large sections of the public and masses of workers no longer have any confidence.

It was generally accepted that nationalization was our most fundamental aim, and countless numbers believed that until production, distribution and exchange were brought under this form of ownership a planned society could not be obtained.

Although this view has now been rejected it still remains an incontrovertible truth.

Political and industrial opponents of nationalization and all forms of public ownership utilized all their vast resources to discredit and prevent any extension of it. That is understandable, but it was never anticipated that nationalization would suffer the heaviest blow from its own erstwhile promoters—the trade union leadership!

To this leadership the preservation of their little trade union empires with their divisions and stupid demarcations proved more important than the success of the nationalized industries, and instead of the workers employed in these industries benefiting from this new form of ownership many have become victims of it.

Labour's political leaders no doubt realized this, because in Labour's 1959 General Election programme there were no proposals for the extension of nationalization and speakers who visited constituencies to support Labour candidates were advised *not to devote much attention to questions of nationalization and public ownership,* as it would lose votes if they did.

Whether or not the Socialist leaders, for reasons of political expediency, thought it advisable to discourage any references to either nationalization or public ownership during the election campaign, it was apparent that the trade union leadership, by its own acts, was responsible for the exclusion of Labour's fundamental aim from the programme itself.

The October 1959 General Election was a turning point in Labour's history. The political leadership turned its back on a Socialist policy not because of its disbelief in such a policy but because the state of trade union affairs made such a policy impracticable.

Social and economic circumstances made public ownership more necessary than ever, but trade union leadership, by clinging to its chaotic and competitive structure, made its application impossible.

The TUC leadership, with whom the Labour Party leaders must always come to terms, had had a choice to make: either to

(1) reconstruct its chaotic and competitive trade union structure and make it possible to extend nationalization and other forms of public ownership; or

(2) preserve its chaotic and competitive structure and abandon all hope of extending nationalization, public ownership or any other form of socialist policy.

It rejected the first choice and clung to the second.

Long before the 1959 General Election the TUC leadership had opposed any reconstruction of the trade unions, even in the industries already nationalized. Again and again it had revealed its preference to preserve the trade union movement as it is, in accord with its nineteenth-century traditions, allowing private enterprise to go on thriving indefinitely.

These leaders represent the true Victorians. They are more conservative than the Tories.

To these trade union leaders the past is heroic, and while the present bewilders them the future frightens them.

History has endowed them with a great heritage. In their rare public speeches they pay tribute to the movement's pioneers and rebels, provided they are dead and secure in their graves.

As these leaders conceive it, the historic mission of the trade union movement and their position as leaders have already been realized. We are living in the best of all possible worlds.

The social furniture is now nicely arranged and anyone seeking to disturb it is a disruptionist or an irresponsible militant and should be sternly disciplined.

The effect of this unchanging and unimaginative leadership has not only destroyed Labour's political prospects but, under this leadership, the trade unions themselves cease to thrive and their influence declines.

In his report for the year 1958 the Chief Registrar of Friendly Societies revealed that while the average union spent on all purposes £2 15s 7d per head, the average contributions of the members during the same year were but £2 15s 3d, which caused Sir Thomas Williamson, of the NUG & MW, to state in the press on December 12, 1959, that 'the situation is so serious that unions are able to carry on only with the aid of income other than contributions, such as interest on investments' which had been accumulated in past years.

Sir Thomas is not the only leader who is worried about 'the unions being run on the cheap'. But nothing is done about it because, as the present competitive, disorderly trade union structure prevents them from establishing the same weekly contributions and the same uniform benefits, each union is afraid to increase its own members' contributions in case they may leave for some other union whose contributions are lower and whose benefits are greater. This leadership, which has devalued trade unionism, is content to look on while more and more TUC affiliates drift into the 'red'.

If anything wants nationalizing it is certainly the trade union contributions and benefits, but the TUC leadership cannot work up any enthusiasm for even that single and essential operation.

The TUC is an anachronism in the modern world. Instead of defeating Labour's opponents it enables them to continue their anti-social rule indefinitely.

The price of TUC leadership is truly incalculable.

CHAPTER 6

DISCREDITING NATIONALIZATION

Long before the conflict over Clause 4 arose Britain possessed several publicly-owned undertakings ranging from Royal Ordnance works, Naval dockyards, postal and telegraph services to municipal undertakings, including a Municipal Bank.

The Tories and Liberals, who were responsible for bringing these undertakings under public ownership, have neither taken steps to extend their activities nor at any time sought to 'denationalize' them.

Even when the 1945 Labour Government carried through its nationalization policy the opposition of the leaders of private enterprise was not based on the principle that all nationalization was evil; it was because the Government's proposals were not limited to 'taking over' the bankrupt and ruined coal mining and railway industries, but also included other industries and services of great profitability as well.

Although the coal owners and railway stockholders would receive generous compensation for the loss of their ruined industries, despite the fact that prior to nationalization they had sustained huge losses, this was no consolation to the financial interests in steel, road haulage, civilian airlines, utility and other profitable undertakings that were to be brought under national ownership.

To these interests the nationalization of coal mines and railways would hardly imperil profits because these two industries, even with Government subsidies, rarely made any. What frightened them was the fact that the Labour Government's nationalization policy went far beyond this. The 'take-over' of electricity and gas was particularly a great shock to them. It deprived them of a rich and ever-expanding field of easy exploitation which they never expected to lose, although their loss has proved to be the people's gain.

In spite of a great extension of these two services and costly

modernization and development programmes, substantial profits
have been earned for use in the national interest, while the price
of both electricity and gas has risen far less than that of other
items that make up the price index.

Nationalization in these two industries alone has proved to be
a great triumph. It has contributed to national stability, and the
consumer, instead of being squeezed to meet the requirements of
private interests, is now assured of an efficient and reliable service at reasonable charges.

It is not at all surprising that the supporters of private enterprise remain implacably opposed to nationalization. As they see
it, the greater its success the greater is their own private loss.

British Airways have shown similar promise, although they
have been severely corroded by the infiltration of aggressive
private interests on the one side and disorderly trade unionism on
the other.

The scandalous events in the steel industry cannot be attributed to any shortcomings of nationalization. They stand to the
shame of those, including the TUC leaders, who, contrary to the
public interest, helped to retrieve this profitable industry for
private enterprise.

And private enterprise in the road haulage industry, after
being paid handsome compensation for its interests in that industry, would never have recovered it if it had not been for divided
trade union forces and an acquiescent leadership.

Even coal mines and railways, in spite of their bankrupt and
obsolete condition when they were taken out of the hands of
their former owners, are rapidly being moulded to meet modern
needs, although at a heavy cost to the miners and the railwaymen.

The short post-war history of nationalization shows that it is
in every way superior to private enterprise, and the political and
industrial leaders of private enterprise, knowing this better than
most people, embarked upon a costly campaign deliberately
designed to misrepresent nationalization, discredit it and, if at all
possible, prevent any extension of it.

In this campaign the anti-nationalizers and their publicists
were most selective. They kept silent about compensation payments; they ignored the great success story of nationalized electricity and the profits made; they did not dwell upon the fact that

the Coal Board had been prohibited from selling coal in a high-priced export market and had had to sell to private industry at home below its economic price; they saw no purpose in enlightening the public on the millions that had to be spent on the reconstruction of the mining industry and the enormous sums that had to be spent on the modernization of an antiquated railway system.

The purpose of the publicists of private enterprise and their backers was not to praise or even report the achievements of nationalization, but to discredit it and poison the minds of the public and uninformed trade unionists against it.

If a nationalized industry, after paying millions of pounds compensation to former owners, sustained a loss, that was publicized with great enthusiasm—minus, of course, any reference to the compensation payments.

To the enemies of nationalization stories about slate in coal, dirty railway carriage windows and trains running late were particularly welcome, and these stories, without any explanation that might have accounted for them, were constantly broadcast in the press and repeated so often by the anti-nationalizers that they became daily topics of conversation.

And all the while this denigrating of nationalization went on and the electors' minds were being conditioned to reject any further nationalization proposals, the TUC leadership looked on and made no serious effort to counter this unscrupulous anti-nationalization campaign. Indeed, if the truth be told, the TUC leadership in many ways assisted the campaign. Even when it has seen fit to issue any statement supporting any particular aspect of nationalization its timing has been such that it has had but little value.

The railway industry was a favourite pre-election target of the anti-nationalizers. They could exploit the losses of this industry; they could trade on the seething discontent amongst the employees and the bitter hostility that for many years had existed between the trade union leaders in this industry.

The victorious Tories on October 8, 1959, must have been grateful to these leaders because they undoubtedly rendered a greater service to the Tory cause than they did to their own.

The accounts of the squabbles and the spiteful exchanges between the leaders of these three main Unions in the railway industry, frequently featured in the press, delighted the Tories but bewildered and angered countless trade unionists and Labour supporters, while the plight of the workers within this nationalized industry grew worse.

Relations between these three Unions were such that one Union would embark upon strike action while the other Unions would remain at work; another rail Union would publicly announce its intention to submit a wage claim, while the other two Unions would publicly announce that they would not. They were only united in their disagreement!

These stoppages and threats of stoppages might have upset and disturbed the commercial life of the country, but to the daily commuters they amounted to periodic torture, which did not endear them to a nationalized industry or to the Labour movement that promoted it—as the results of the 1959 General Election showed.

In that election Harold Hutchinson, of the *Daily Herald*, claims that 3,000,000 trade unionists lined up with the Tories. In the light of the propaganda of the anti-nationalizers on the one hand and the failure of the trade union leaders to practice what they preached on the other, it is surprising that the Tories did not reap an even greater harvest than they did!

In the pre-nationalization period none was more vociferous in the advocacy for a planned, co-ordinated transport system than were the leaders of the three main railway Unions. They all favoured the elimination of the separate railway companies, such as the GWR, LMS, LNER and the Southern Railway, but they took care to ensure the preservation of their own separate, competing trade union outfits.

What was sauce for the capitalist goose was too tart for the trade union gander. As a consequence nationalization in the railway industry, from its very beginning, started at a great disadvantage.

In an industry whose operations were now co-ordinated under a central Transport Executive an united railway labour force was essential, yet the trade union bosses insisted upon keeping this labour force divided up into three Unions, each of which pursued a different policy from the others.[1]

---

[1] In the railway workshops and ancillary services, all part of the railway industry, there are upwards of fifty other trade unions in addition to these three major ones!

Instead of being an effective partner in railway management and development; instead of exercising control over redundancy and establishing effective joint consultation and ensuring that 'those who willed the end should provide the means' to pay adequate wages, these three discordant Unions fought amongst themselves, and the railwaymen, instead of benefiting from nationalization, became victims of it.

Amongst countless numbers of railwaymen, to the delight of the anti-nationalizers, nationalization became a term of derision, and in their thousands they left the railways for other occupations; there is no doubt that many of these resentful workers and their wives helped to swell the Tory vote on October 8, 1959.

If there is any doubt about the abject failure of trade union leadership in the railway industry Lord Lucas's speech in the House of Lords on December 17, 1959, and the Guillebaud Report published on March 4, 1960, will remove that doubt.

The role of the trade unions in the railway industry will continue to be a pathetic and subservient one until the labour force is united under the control of a single trade union Executive instead of numerous separate ones.

Even in the recent dispute it was neither the TUC leaders nor the railway leaders, but the threatened action of the 'fed up' London and Manchester railworkers that caused Sir Brian Robertson to give a pledge that if the independent review of wages (which had been going on for eighteen months) recommended higher wages he would be prepared to negotiate interim rises back-dated to January 11, 1960.

This statement, which the national press on January 12, 1960, described as 'unique', does not reflect the effectiveness of the trade union leadership, because Sir Brian made this promise without troubling to consult the Unions about it at all.

As the leaders of the three railway Unions occupy privileged seats on the TUC General Council that are not the subject of ballot, it may be wondered whether the TUC leadership approves of the continuation of the present trade union divisions in the railway industry?

The record shows that the TUC General Council—the leadership—has never disapproved of the divisions in the railway industry, and it has certainly never made any attempt to remove them.

At the 1955 Southport Congress the TUC leadership certainly had the opportunity to make its position clear on the subject of trade union conflict in both the railway industry and the other nationalized industries, because on that occasion a motion in the following terms was tabled by the National Union of Public Employees for consideration (page 443, 1955 Congress Report):

This Congress realizes that as the establishment of the nationalized industries and services, which Congress so vigorously promoted, has resulted in the elimination of the competitive units, the creation of an integrated, centrally controlled administration and the national determination of wages and conditions of those employed in those industries and services, it is desirable in the interests of those engaged in the said industries and services, and to ensure the success and furtherance of nationalization, that steps be taken to eliminate competitive trade unionism therein, by the creation of an integrated trade union in each of the nationalized industries and services, under a single Executive Council.

Accordingly, it instructs the General Council to conduct an inquiry as to the way in which this may best be achieved. As such integration will largely depend upon the co-operation of the many existing unions, Congress requests the General Council to consult those unions and, in particular, to consider with them whether one representative union in each of the nationalized industries and services would prove superior to any form of working agreement among separate unions.

The findings of such an inquiry, together with the views of the unions that would be affected thereby, to be submitted to the 1956 Congress.

This motion gave the TUC leadership an excellent opportunity to do something really constructive in the newly nationalized industries by removing the trade union friction that was retarding the successful development of these industries.

Unfortunately, and not for the first time, the TUC leadership decisively rejected this opportunity and advised Congress to vote against the motion. On this occasion the TUC leadership selected the genial Sir Tom O'Brien to advise Congress to cast out the motion which sought to bring about trade union reorganization in the nationalized industries.

In support of such advice Sir Tom declared:

The TUC General Council believe that the time is not yet ripe for the General Council themselves to undertake such a far reaching inquiry into the nationalized industries. We do not by any means condemn the spirit contained in the motion . . . but I cannot ask Congress to support it, but on the contrary I ask Congress to reject it.

Mr Jim Haworth, leader of one of the railway Unions (TSSA), was also anxious to oppose the motion. He said:

I doubt whether anyone can quarrel with the principle of this motion—the principle may be good, but we have to take note of the right time, and I want to suggest that this is not the right time to have the suggested inquiry, or to try to bring about one union in each of the nationalized industries. (1955 Congress Report, 444-5.)

Congress accepted the advice the TUC leadership expressed through Sir Tom O'Brien that 'the time was not ripe', and that of Mr Jim Haworth that 'it was not the right time', and threw the motion out.

That was in 1955—five years ago—and trade union chaos in the nationalized industries is even more acute now than it was then, but the time is still 'not yet ripe' and the 'right time' has still not arrived, in spite of the fact that since this 1955 motion was rejected the bitterness between the three rail Unions (NUR, ASLE & F and TSSA) has reached such intensity that the relations between warring tribes would appear more friendly, while the position of the railwaymen becomes more and more degraded.

The exodus of underpaid, ill-treated and resentful employees continues, and the *News Chronicle* (January 12, 1960) was able to report that over a period of but twelve weeks for which figures were available a further 10,000 railwaymen resigned.

In this nationalized industry, where three conflicting Unions claim to represent and protect the workers, they saw no future and left it.

Railwaymen are seasoned trade unionists, but how many of the 10,000 men who resigned their jobs, and the hundreds of thousands more who were declared redundant and 'put on the stones' without any proper compensation, will retain their trade union faith and their trade union membership in those other industries where it is hoped they will find a more considerate employer and a more effective trade union leadership?

Instead of the united efforts and combined resources of the three rail Unions being utilized to ensure that the workers in this nationalized industry receive treatment not inferior to that received by workers in other industries, their leaders prefer to keep them divided to enable them to go on crowing from their own little dunghills.

The *Daily Herald*, to its credit, has done much to help the depressed railwaymen. In addition to drawing attention to the disagreements between the three Unions, the *Herald* correspondent Deryck Winterton printed a series of moving letters he had received from many railwaymen. Here is one he published on January 4, 1960:

I am a railwayman with twenty-seven years' service, the last nineteen as a goods guard. I enclose my pay slip for the week ending December 12, 1959. This shows my gross earnings as £10 19s 1d. (Net £9 16s 3d.)

To get this 'magnificent' reward, here is what I had to do. My signing-on times were as follows:

				Overtime
December	7	Monday	2.25 a.m.	Nil
December	8	Tuesday	2.05 a.m.	1 hr.
December	9	Wednesday	2.05 a.m.	2 hrs. 25 mins.
December	10	Thursday	2.05 a.m.	Nil
December	11	Friday	2.05 a.m.	Nil
December	12	Saturday	Day off	

My overtime for the week amounted to £1 0s 5d—to compensate me for getting out of bed at 1 a.m. every day.

Can you tell me of any other man in industry who would go to bed every night for a week around 7 p.m. to get up at 1 a.m. (this means Sunday evening, too) for a pound a week extra?

Weather conditions that week were not of the best, for we had fog, rain and gales blowing almost every night. I had to cycle two miles each way (no public transport after 1.30 a.m.).

Apart from my duties as a guard, I had the pleasure of walking from one station to another at 5 a.m.—a mere 50 minutes' walk each day.

And for all this I received £9 16s 3d as my pay slip shows.

We wonder whether this unfortunate fellow believes, with Sir Tom O'Brien, the TUC leader, that 'the time is not yet ripe', or with Mr Jim Haworth, TSSA leader, that 'it is not the right time'.

If the anti-nationalizers failed to influence many of these good trade unionists to vote Tory on October 8, 1959, the incredible actions of a disunited trade union leadership in the rail industry may well have succeeded.

CHAPTER 7

CONDITIONING THE ELECTORS

The TUC leadership at the 1950 Brighton Congress presented its considered views on 'The Public Ownership of Industry'. In this statement, under a bold sub-head—'Increased Industrial Democracy'—the leadership affirmed:

that public ownership makes possible a great extension of the part that the workpeople can play in the running of the industries in which they are employed. It can provide the machinery for joint consultation at all levels and training facilities to make promotion open to all . . . (1950 Brighton Congress Report, page 566.)

It is perfectly true that the public ownership (or nationalization) of industries can make it possible for the workers to play a greater part in the running of these industries and enjoy facilities denied to them under private enterprise—provided that within such industries private enterprise is effectively curbed and competitive trade unions are completely eliminated.

Unfortunately, since the TUC leadership presented the statement quoted above, it has lamentably failed to establish the necessary conditions in the nationalized industries to ensure 'Increased Industrial Democracy', and until the present TUC is substituted by a more enlightened one it is doubtful if such a democracy will ever be realized.

Throughout these industries, instead of private enterprise steadily declining and the trade unions taking on more important roles, the reverse has taken place. Private enterprise has become more powerful and prosperous, while the trade unions have become more competitive and less effective.

It is true that in the coal mining industry coal is now mined under public control, but this control is still dependent on private enterprise for its vast supplies of mining and engineering equipment, as well as upon private distributive services. It is also true that nationalized railways provide, at a loss, the main product, 'transport', but private enterprise, at a considerable profit, supplies the locomotives, diesel engines, wagons and a thousand and one other things.

In each and every one of the nationalized industries there is an extensive area in which private enterprise continues to expand and flourish, and in some instances it has been aided by Government grants and subsidies at the expense of the nationalized industries themselves.

It would be unrealistic to expect that overnight private enterprise should be wiped out. Even in developing nationalized or publicly-owned industries private enterprise has its place. But what is contrary to original expectation is that private enterprise, acting as chandlers to the nationalized industries, is expanding more rapidly and commanding a higher rate of profit than it ever did in its pre-nationalization days.

Even in the nationalized sphere of civil airways private enterprise is in the lead. Over a six-year period ended on March 31, 1959, the volume of traffic in the nationalized BOAC increased by only 64%, while for the same period the volume of traffic carried by the private airlines increased by 385%.

Unfortunately the TUC leadership has shown little interest in the affairs of the nationalized industries. It is clear from our researches that it has never sought to encourage the nationalized industries to meet their own supply needs whenever and wherever they can, nor has the TUC leadership made the slightest attempt to remove the competitive and disorderly trade unionism which has brought discredit upon nationalization and made the creation of 'Increased Industrial Democracy' impossible.

Since the 1950 Brighton Congress, under the present TUC leadership, the high hopes possessed by millions of trade unionists in the immediate post-war years have been shattered. Many of them have now lost all confidence in nationalization and in the Labour movement that promoted it. There is a great deal of information available to show this trend, apart from the disastrous results of the 1959 General Election, yet whenever the TUC leadership has had the opportunity to do something to reverse this unfortunate development it has shirked it.

At the 1955 Southport Congress, as is shown in the previous chapter, the TUC leadership advised the rejection of a proposal that called upon the leadership to 'take steps to eliminate competitive trade unionism and create an integrated trade union in each of the nationalized services under a single Union Executive Council'.

At the 1957 Blackpool Congress a further plea was made stressing the need for the reorganization of the trade union movement. The late Jim Campbell, who was so conscious of the trade union disorder in his own railway industry, then moved a motion in the following terms:

This Congress welcomes the statements of prominent trade union leaders stressing the need for a reconstruction of the trade union movement. It believes that much can be done to improve our trade union structure to the great benefit of the membership. Congress therefore instructs the General Council to conduct a survey and to make recommendations to the 1958 Congress designed to assist in any reorganization necessary. Further, Congress realizes that in any such contemplated reconstruction the interests of the trade union officers and staffs should be protected. (1957 Congress Report, page 331.)

The motion was seconded by a representative of the National Union of Public Employees. It was supported by the National Union of Mineworkers, the Tobacco Workers' Union and the Amalgamated Union of Building Trades Workers. Opposition was forthcoming from the General Secretary of the Railway Clerks (who is also a member of the TUC leadership), the President of the ASLE & F (who is also a member of the TUC leadership) and the TUC General Secretary, Sir Vincent Tewson.

Sir Vincent's speech, recorded in the official report, indicated pretty clearly that the leadership had no intentions of disturbing the present TUC set-up or embarking upon any reconstruction of the outmoded and competitive trade unions. In retrospect, it all looked pretty good to him, and in any case the services of the leadership were always at the disposal of the affiliated Unions!

Sir Vincent made that clear when he measured the needs of the present with the report of the 1924 Inquiry—thirty-six years ago. He went on to say:

The 1924 inquiry resulted in a final report in 1927. In 1924 we began a three years' task. It would not be a three years' task on the next occasion, it is true, because I think there is very little—and I think Congress is convinced of this—that the General Council could add to the recommendations which they made in their last report. But the matter is still under review and if there are any unions, as

E

was said in 1955, which would like the assistance of the General
Council in being brought together for purposes of getting closer
unity, again, as in all things, the services of the General Council are
at the disposal of affiliated organizations. The motion is unrealistic
and should be turned down. (1957 Congress Report, page 337.)

This moderate motion, which Sir Vincent advised was 'unrealistic and should be turned down', simply asked the TUC
leadership itself 'to conduct a survey into our trade union affairs
and make recommendations designed to assist any reorganization
necessary'.

It may appear strange to the uninitiated that the leadership
should refuse to conduct such an inquiry, particularly as the
inquiry would be in its own hands. But it is not so strange when
it is realized what an intriguing problem such an inquiry
presents to the TUC leadership.

The TUC leadership itself is representative of conflicting union
interests—craft, general, industrial unions and so on—and were
the representatives of these groups to undertake an examination
of the prevailing trade union structure they could not produce
any sensible report that did not provide for the abandonment of
these conflicting groups. Because the leadership realized what
the inevitable consequences of such an inquiry would be it
refused to undertake it.

A leadership that on account of considerations of its own
interests cannot or refuses to effect structural changes in respect
of itself or its affiliated Unions cannot possibly perform any
effective role in our industrial affairs. It becomes irresponsible
and no longer has a useful mission to serve. Instead of assisting
and guiding the workers, it bewilders, confuses and misleads
them.

The strikes and industrial disturbances in the pre-election
year, which assured the Tories of their third consecutive victory,
were not due to 'irresponsible shop stewards' but were the out-
ward and visible signs of the massive failure of trade union
leadership.

One of the many strikes that inflicted irreparable harm to the
trade union cause and seriously damaged Labour's General
Election effort, was the London Airport strike, which lasted
eight days, involved 4,000 employees, grounded the entire fleet

of the nationalized BOAC, cost £999,000 and, believe it or not, involved seventeen trade unions.

The public was bewildered and angered by the contradictory statements made by the leaders of the seventeen Unions as to the causes of the strike, while the passengers, the immediate victims of it who were prevented from travelling to their destinations in various parts of the world, suffered great hardship and extreme inconvenience, which is hardly likely to endear them to the nationalized BOAC.

The only people whose feelings could not be gauged were the TUC leaders. As in many previous disputes, these leaders did not intervene and they kept silent. Even if seventeen competitive Unions were feuding among themselves, making effective negotiation impossible, inflicting damage on the cause of trade unionism and injuring the interests of a nationalized service, the TUC leadership saw no reason to step in.

Although the stoppage was undermining British prestige at home and abroad and driving still more former Labour supporters into the Tory camp, the TUC leaders remained unmoved. They depended, so it seemed, on the forces of attrition settling the strike for them, and if, eventually, there were to be an inquiry into the dispute it would be a public inquiry in which the TUC leadership, as such, would not be involved.

The TUC leadership did not concern itself with this eight days' struggle, nor did the national leaders of the seventeen trade unions intervene. They kept out of it and left this ruinous dispute to their non-commissioned officers to do the best they could.

It might well be that the BOAC management had provoked the employees by threats of redundancy and by long delays in settling their complaints, but these grievances would hardly have arisen if there had been but one or two trade unions at London Airport instead of seventeen of them.

The trade union leaders who, after ten years of nationalization in this industry, allowed this appalling trade union disorder to continue cannot exonerate themselves from responsibility for this regrettable strike which did so much damage to our trade union cause and our political prospects.

When it was finally settled an inquiry was held, but it was conducted by Professor Jack and not by the TUC.

The inquiry lasted seven days. It supplied the newspapers

with a most unedifying and sensational account of trade union relations and their internal affairs. Trade unionism was seriously damaged, nationalization was brought into further discredit and the prospects of a Tory election victory greatly increased.

And the TUC leadership looked on!

Even the lengthy bell-ringing dispute at Briggs, which put thousands of men out of work, did not succeed in arousing the interest of the TUC leadership. This was another gift to the Tories. The revelations during the course of the dispute did much harm to the Labour movement and generated much public mistrust in trade union intentions.

In this one undertaking the extent of trade union disorder can be gauged by the fact that no less than twenty-two Unions had members who became involved in the dispute. Here again, as in the London Airport strike, none of the twenty-two Union Executives had the right or the power to intervene. In the trade union chaos at Briggs the Union Executives must either act in unison or not act at all. They chose the latter course, and, as in numerous previous disputes, the non-commissioned officers were left in control.

We intend no criticism of the NCOs, because in the present trade union disorder at Briggs and elsewhere they are indispensable and without them relations between employers and employees would be completely impossible. We address our criticism to the TUC leadership for allowing such a state of affairs to arise.

At Briggs the TUC had every justification and a splendid opportunity to institute an inquiry into trade union affairs in this undertaking, and to do something to remove the friction that twenty-two competing Unions must inevitably cause.

But again the TUC leadership shirked its obligation to do this. It kept outside the ring. We had to suffer yet another Public Inquiry. This time it was conducted by Lord Cameron, and it proved to be a more damaging exposure of trade union affairs than even the Professor Jack Inquiry.

The Cameron Report delighted the Tory Central Office. It provided Tory canvassers with excellent ammunition. It enabled them to portray the trade unions as being incapable of handling their own affairs and to warn the electors how ruinous it would be if they supported Labour's policy of nationalization.

The right to strike is a precious possession, and the movement must never relinquish its right to use it. But in present circumstances there is no semblance of central trade union control or direction and a woeful lack of co-ordination between one Union and another, and unless great care is exercised those who wish to deprive the workers of the right to strike may have the opportunity to do so, with the blessing of the TUC leaders themselves.

The London bus strike was a great epic. It lasted six weeks and the 50,000 busmen and their families, without wages for that period, endured great hardship. Whatever the merits of this dispute may be, it proved to be a tragic commentary on the mismanagement of our trade union affairs.

While the bus Union leader (and a member of the TUC leadership) kept the buses off the London streets in order to secure a modest wage increase for his members, the railway Union leader (and also a member of the TUC leadership) directed his members to keep the trains running below the London streets!

This was a remarkable example of trade union co-ordination, which no doubt was difficult for the defeated busmen, as well as their wives, to appreciate.

There were enormous political reactions to this struggle which on October 8, 1959, must have proved gratifying to the Tory Party.

We wonder whether the special nineteen-member committee which the TUC leadership has set up to ascertain the causes of official and unofficial strikes approved the action of the striking busmen or the 'blacklegging' railwaymen!

And what of the strike at Jaguars of Coventry in April 1959, when the political parties were drafting their General Election programmes? What was the great issue on this occasion?

It was over the membership of a youth. He was already a member of one Union, but another Union in the same factory demanded that he should be a member of theirs. This little scrap caused 4,000 men to be thrown idle, with a loss of pay of £50,000.

If the consequences of trade union disorder in the nationalized railway industry, at London Airport, at Briggs and elsewhere were not sufficient to convert the doubting voters, the numerous demarcation disputes and the battles between Unions as to who should twang the string or bore the holes would certainly bring them into the Tory camp.

We should not complain that 3,000,000 trade unionists lined up with the Tories. They deserted us because they had lost faith in us, and responsibility for this is largely due to irresponsible trade union leadership.

These are hard words but the circumstances fully justify them. We are to be saddled with Tory rule for at least ten to fifteen years, which may be extended indefinitely. This is not due to the merits of Toryism or the cleverness of Tory leaders, but to the failure of our own.

And there is little likelihood of anything being done to retrieve the position. Trade union disorder will be allowed to continue. The TUC General Council will be content to repeat meaningless phrases about 'closer trade union unity', to condemn wild-cat strikes at its monthly meetings and to leave things just as they are, or much worse, until the next General Election comes round, when we are likely to get a bigger beating than we had on October 8, 1959.

Of course, TUC leaders will, on appropriate occasions, give lip service to the policy of extending nationalization or public ownership, knowing full well that without a reconstruction of the trade unions it cannot be realized.

We deceive ourselves when we advocate the social ownership of either the whole or a part of the engineering industry. In this industry there are now upwards of a hundred different Unions operating. In the Confederation of Engineering Unions alone there are no less than thirty-nine Unions.

These conflicting and competing Unions produce enough chaos under private enterprise. What the results would be under social ownership it is difficult to imagine. Perhaps that's why the TUC leaders have such little faith in social ownership.

Without a single responsible trade union Executive being in control of each industry, and the TUC General Council exercising real central authority conditioned on a real democratic basis instead of the present spurious one, Labour's political success will never be assured and our trade union ideals will never be realized.

CHAPTER 8

AN UNPRECEDENTED PLEDGE

We believe that the TUC leadership in its present form and as now constituted will never make it possible for Labour, whoever its political leaders may be, to achieve another enduring electoral victory.

To have allowed nationalization to be dirtied and discredited; to have permitted trade union disorder to play such havoc with industrial relations and to stand idly aside while acute hardships are inflicted on members of the public, as well as upon workers thrown idle and deprived of wages without even being consulted, makes it unlikely that the TUC leadership will ever command sufficient support again from either the public or the workers.

It is, of course, possible that the Tory Government may commit some really stupid acts and fall into such public disfavour as to enable Labour to defeat it. In such event Labour's victory is not likely to be more than a fleeting one, because the leadership of the TUC, over many years, has produced such an unhealthy industrial situation and such a mental climate that it would be impossible for a Labour Government to endure.

But not only is it unlikely that the present TUC leadership will ever regain the confidence it has lost; there are other disgraceful and indelible marks on its record, including:

(1) The unprecedented pledge to the Tory Government in 1951;

(2) Its decision reached, without the knowledge of Congress, to assist the Tory Government to denationalize the steel industry; and

(3) Its deliberate act of evading the public ownership mandates of its own Congress.

We propose to deal with the last two items later. Here we refer to the amazing pledge which the TUC leadership presented to the Tory Government after they had won the General Election on October 25, 1951.

It is pretty generally conceded that democratic government in Britain is dependent upon two major parties and, above all, on an effective opposition. These things, however, seem to be of little importance to the TUC leadership. After the 1951 election, instead of assisting the Labour Party (now the official Opposition) to do everything possible to preserve the great achievements of the Labour Government over the previous six years (1945-1951), and exercise the maximum restraint over the acquisitive-minded Tories, the TUC leaders were already kneeling down to wash their feet.

Almost immediately after the October 1951 General Election, and within a week of the votes being counted, the TUC leadership, in a public statement unprecedented in trade union history, made a declaration of fealty to the victorious Tory Government.

While Labour supporters were still licking their wounds, and before our canvassers had recovered from their arduous but unsuccessful endeavours to defeat the Tories, they received the TUC *coup de grâce*, which affirmed that the TUC would—

seek to work amicably with whatever Government is in power and, through consultation jointly with Ministers . . . to find practical solutions to the social and economic problems facing this country. There need be no doubt, therefore, of the attitude of the TUC towards the new Government. In joint consultations and in all other activities it will be our constant aim and duty to ensure the steady progress and betterment of the general condition of Britain and of our people. We shall continue in that duty under a Conservative Government.

This statement, which was issued by the TUC leadership soon after the polling booths had closed, was also reproduced on page 300 of the 1952 Margate Congress Report. It revealed that in the minds of the TUC leaders a victorious Tory Government was as good as a defeated Labour Government any day, and that the TUC, in co-operation with the Tories, would be able to '*find practical solutions to the social and economic problems facing this country*'.

It showed that the defeat of the Labour Government was of little consequence as, together, the TUC and the Tories would be able to deal effectively with all the problems facing us.

It was not anticipated that the TUC leaders should call a general strike for the purpose of throwing the Tories out, but it was hardly expected that they would issue a statement of such a character at such an ill-chosen time, that could only create bewilderment and confusion in the minds of millions of Labour supporters.

What was the motive that prompted the TUC leaders to make such a declaration? Was it an indication of the stranger things that were soon to follow, to which they had already committed themselves?

Anyway, this TUC declaration warmed the hearts of the Tory Ministers; the City could not restrain its enthusiasm, while newspaper editors went into rhapsodies about 'the good sense of the practical-minded men in charge of the trade union movement'.

The Tories regarded it as the 'all clear' for them to proceed with their plans to redeem their scandalous promises to give back to the steel magnates and the road operators the industries which the Labour Government had taken from them.

The pledge of the TUC leaders to 'work *amicably*' with the Tory Government '*in order to find practical solutions to the social and economic problems facing the country*' was soon to be redeemed, and the drift of trade unionists from their allegiance to the Labour Party began.

At this critical moment the policy of the Labour Party contrasted sharply with the TUC's policy of 'amicability'.

The Labour Party in forthright pronouncements declared that if in fact the Tories did denationalize steel and road haulage, for which they had no clear mandate, the Labour Party would restore them at the first opportunity.

The TUC leadership preserved a significant silence. This silence continued until after the decisive event of the adoption of the Queen's Speech.

To that Address the Labour Party spokesman, Mr George Strauss, unsuccessfully moved the Party's amendment, which stated:

But humbly regret that the Glorious Speech contains proposals relating to the iron and steel industry and road haulage which will not assist the national effort, but will cause anxiety and uncertainty in two vital industries.

While Labour's Parliamentary spokesman condemned the Tories for 'disregarding the national interests and damaging the national economy' by their unscrambling policy, the Tory Minister of Supply, Mr Sandys, was showering praise on the statesmanship of the TUC leadership!

But in the years that followed did the TUC leaders, in amicable consultation with the Tory Government, 'find practical solutions to the social and economic problems facing this country'? Were any communiqués issued over the joint signatures of the Government and the TUC leaders announcing, say, the abolition of unemployment, decent pensions for the aged and that rents should not be raised?

Unfortunately we have no knowledge that any decisions were reached at all. The TUC leaders did, hopefully and regularly, send an SOS to the Tory Chancellor on the eve of his Budget Speeches, but these never found their way into the Budget Box.

By this amazing act of fealty the TUC leaders had cheapened themselves and cheapened the movement as well.

Later, in 1954, there had been a serious dispute in the engineering industry that had led to another Court of Inquiry. The then Tory Minister of Labour no doubt thought that the creation of a supra-national Advisory Board, composed of employers and trade union representatives, would appeal to the TUC leaders. The Minister thought that such a supra-national Advisory Board would be able to give advice or take some sort of action to prevent labour stoppages when normal negotiations failed. (Page 239, Brighton 1954 Congress Report.)

Here was a chance for the TUC leaders 'in amicable consultations to find practical solutions to the social and economic problems facing the country'. Did they take the chance? They rejected it out of hand. Tackling concrete problems of such a character has no attraction for them.

In August 1957 the Tory Government appointed a three-man Council on Prices, Productivity and Incomes under the chairmanship of Lord Cohen. Here was another opportunity for the TUC leadership to participate in 'amicable consultation' with the Tory Government. It was an opportunity to do even more than that: it could have adumbrated and publicized its views on every aspect of the economy, but, unsportingly, the TUC leadership not only refused to participate in any amicable consultation but also opposed the establishment of the Cohen Committee.

But on this occasion the TUC leadership was divided. One

section of the leadership became quite militant, declaring that 'it could publicize its views on the Government's economic policy without meeting the Cohen Council', while the other section of the leadership pleaded that 'a refusal to meet the Cohen Council would be damaging to the trade union movement' (page 280, Bournemouth 1958 Congress Report).

But the negative section of the TUC leadership won the day. The Cohen Committee was ignored.

It would seem that in an inquiry into prices, productivity and incomes promoted by the Tory Government it would be improper, and certainly contrary to the spirit of amicability, if the TUC leadership were to disturb the academic atmosphere of the Cohen Committee by drawing attention to the plight of the underpaid railwaymen and the ill-treated agricultural workers, and exposing the blatant inequities of basing wage rates on the least economic and the least profitable units of the various industries, which are so productive of labour unrest.

Although the TUC leaders ignored this Committee they did not withdraw their pledge 'to go on working amicably with the Tory Government to find practical solutions to the social and economic problems facing this country', and we shall never know their great achievements!

All we do know is that this amazing pledge lost the TUC leaders the respect of countless trade unionists and only succeeded in commanding the contempt of the Tories.

With good reason, the Sunday Observer, on October 11, 1959, had this to say:

There was a time when the Tories were terrified of the TUC, and thought they could not govern unless they could rely on its neutrality. But not now. Even before they were returned, Ministers had come to feel a slight contempt for the members of the TUC and their pretensions.

The Government still went through the motions of consulting them, but for a long time Ministers have not taken them seriously. No sooner had the door of No. 10 closed behind Sir Tom O'Brien and Sir Vincent Tewson than their memoranda were dropped into the waste-paper basket. Never, in fact, has the influence of the TUC been so low as during the past twelve months.

CHAPTER 9

1952 MARGATE CONGRESS

TUC LEADERSHIP RELUCTANT TO ACCEPT
PUBLIC OWNERSHIP MANDATE

While the Tories, encouraged by the promise of the TUC to work amicably with them, were busily drafting the Bills to de-nationalize the steel and road haulage industries and constituting the Boards to give effect to them, the 1952 Margate Congress fell due.

The highlight of this Congress was the debate on public ownership. It arose on a composite motion moved by the National Union of Public Employees, seconded by the Association of Engineering and Shipbuilding Draughtsmen and supported by the National Union of Mineworkers, the Amalgamated Union of Foundry Workers and the Chemical Workers' Union.

This composite motion sought to extend public ownership, and was in the following terms:

This Congress notes the intention of the Tory Government to de-nationalize the Road Haulage and Iron and Steel industries and declares its support of the Trade Unions directly concerned and the Labour Movement generally in their resistance to this reactionary anti-working class procedure. It endorses the declared intention of the Labour Party to renationalize these industries.

Congress reaffirms its faith in the principles of social ownership, but recognizes that if their application remains restricted to a limited number of industries and services the full advantage of social ownership will be lost. It therefore welcomes the Labour Party's declaration that it will extend social ownership.

Congress therefore calls upon the General Council to formulate proposals for the extension of public ownership to other industries and services, particularly those now subject to monopoly control, such proposals to have due regard to the 'Plan for Engineering' of the Confederation of Shipbuilding and Engineering Unions and other proposals submitted by affiliated organizations. Congress further calls upon the General Council to formulate general proposals for the democratization of the nationalized industries and services calculated to make possible the ultimate realization of full industrial democracy.

These proposals shall be submitted to the 1953 Congress, and, after endorsement, presented to the political wing of our Movement, for inclusion in Labour's General Election programme. (1952 Margate Congress Report, pages 438-48.)

During the speeches of the mover, seconder and supporters of this composite motion it was soon made apparent that although it was but a reiteration of past decisions of Congress it was, on this occasion, commanding exceptional support from the delegates present.

Usually the TUC leadership depends upon its colleagues (also members of the General Council) who choose to sit with their delegations to 'guide' the Congress delegates, which allows those leaders who prefer to sit on the platform to display an attitude of apparent neutrality, in the confident hope that no unwelcome policies will be adopted by Congress. But this time it was not to be. The delegates knew what they wanted and were determined to get it.

There was no vocal opposition to the proposed composite motion, although it was known that the attitude of the leadership was not a favourable one. Those who sat on the platform not only preserved complete silence but also appeared glued to their seats while the President (the late Mr Arthur Deakin) eagerly scanned their ranks hoping to find some of them trying to 'catch his eye', but no one gave any sign that he wished to be called upon to speak.

As the noise and excitement in Congress grew, the President called on Mr Charles Geddes, one of the most able members of the leadership, to reply on behalf of the General Council to the promoters of the composite, hoping no doubt that he would succeed in persuading the delegates not to commit the General Council to the public ownership policy as set out in the composite motion.

Mr Geddes rose at the President's direction. He admitted that:

This is one of those resolutions which put Congress, and incidentally the General Council, in the greatest difficulty.

There is little between the General Council and the speakers who have been in the rostrum in support of the composite.

He would agree that it would be difficult, almost impossible, for Congress to reject it.

It is the mechanics of the resolution that present the difficulty.

It would take time, too much time. We will have to survey every industry in this country to establish priorities.

Then we would have to determine how many and which industries should be nationalized.

And you have given us only until next Congress. It is a quite impossible task.

Concluding, Mr Geddes stated that the General Council could not take on this job. 'We just can't do it.' But the General Council 'won't bury it'.

It was then for the mover of the composite motion to close the debate. In doing so he assured Mr Geddes that if the General Council could not finish the job by next year's Congress it could produce a progress report and let Congress see how it was getting on.

Besides, if the General Council did not accept the motion it would give the Government the 'green light' to go on with its reactionary policy of denationalizing the steel and road haulage industries.

During these exchanges excitement mounted on the floor of Congress. Although the debate had been concluded the President seemed unwilling to put the issue to the vote, and the excitement turned to general uproar.

One noted industrial correspondent wrote in his paper that he 'had not seen anything like it in over twenty years of TUC reporting'.

While the President consulted Sir Vincent Tewson and his assistant, Mr George Woodcock, the delegates stamped and shouted. After this consultation the President, quite contrary to accepted procedure and without the approval of the promoters of the motion, announced his intention not to take a vote for or against the motion (which is the normal procedure), but instead he would ask Congress to decide whether or not it should be submitted to the General Council for consideration.

Protests came from all over the hall at this questionable ruling, and the noise from the shouting, whistling and stamping of the delegates rose to a tumult.

Finally the platform capitulated. Now, in a silence that could almost be felt, the President put the motion to Congress, and after the count had been completed he announced that the motion had been carried by 4,542,000 votes, to the almost riotous delight of the delegates.

It was truly a memorable occasion. It was thought that the TUC leadership, in spite of its obvious dislike of this public owner-ship proposal which Congress had adopted by such a decisive vote, would honour this mandate and prepare preliminary plans for submission to the 1953 Congress for the consideration of the delegates, preparatory to 'FORMULATING PROPOSALS FOR THE EXTENSION OF PUBLIC OWNERSHIP FOR PRESENTATION TO THE POLITICAL WING OF THE MOVEMENT, FOR INCLUSION IN LABOUR'S GENERAL ELECTION PROGRAMME', in accordance with the terms of this 1952 resolution.

But it did not work out that way. Events were to show that the TUC leadership had no intention of implementing the wishes of the 1952 Margate Congress.

In the debate Mr Geddes had frankly stated that plans for the extension of public ownership could not be prepared by the General Council in time for the 1953 Congress. He said that was 'a quite impossible task'.

Mr Geddes was quite right. The TUC leadership was not only unable, or unwilling, to prepare preliminary plans during the year from 1952 to 1953: it also failed to do it in the seven following years right up to 1959!

During these seven years the trade union movement was deceived, and when Labour's General Election programme was distributed to the electors in the 1959 General Election the 'policies' referred to in that programme in respect of our indus-trial affairs not only disregarded the public ownership mandate of successive Congresses but were in direct opposition to those mandates.

In the following chapters we shall show how the TUC leader-ship carried out its pledge to work amicably with the Tory Government, and how, without the authority of Congress, it appointed TUC leaders to assist in the denationalization of the steel industry.

As the TUC draws no distinction between the terms 'social ownership' and 'public ownership', such terms throughout this book are regarded as synonymous.

CHAPTER 10

TUC LEADERSHIP IGNORES 1952 CONGRESS MANDATE

AND ASSISTS TORY GOVERNMENT TO DENATIONALIZE THE STEEL INDUSTRY

The Tory Government introduced its Bill to denationalize the iron and steel industries in November 1952, and it received the Royal Assent in May 1953. The Steel Board, upon which the TUC agreed to be represented, was then constituted to deal with the unscrambling process.

The importance of these events and their impact on the Labour movement are likely to increase rather than diminish as the years pass.

The action of the TUC leadership in committing itself to assist the Tory Government to hand back the steel industry to private enterprise may prove to be the greatest disaster the movement has yet sustained, and future trade union historians may well conclude that during the second half of this century Labour's internal conflicts, its prolonged and unparalleled defeat and its decline are not unconnected with the amazing and unjustifiable act of surrender and abject submission by this TUC leadership in 1953.

History shows that when, owing to temporary circumstances, people are unable to practise their beliefs, they don't change them. In hope, they cling to their beliefs without compromising themselves or their creed. The TUC leadership had no such faith, and as a result instead of the year 1953 being recalled with pride it will be remembered with shame.

It seems incredible that, without the consent or knowledge of Congress, the TUC leaders, at an unrepresentative meeting of the General Council, should have approved the appointment of three of their own TUC colleagues as members of the newly constituted Steel Board whose specific purpose was to bring about the denationalization of an industry already nationalized. Sir Lincoln Evans was to be Vice-Chairman of the Board.

In September 1952 Congress had mandated the TUC leaders to seek an extension of nationalization. Now, a few months later, they were pursuing a deliberate policy of curtailing it.

What a stimulant this was to the Tories! Nationalization must really stink when prominent trade union leaders, with the blessing of the TUC General Council, undertook, at high salaries, the job of demolishing it.

Tory editors, in their newspapers, gave the 'full treatment' to these happenings. They were jubilant in the knowledge that the TUC leaders had come to the rescue of private enterprise and that countless electors would never again be influenced as to the advantages of social ownership and a planned economy, which was the basis of Labour's programme.

In the eyes of the public the TUC leaders themselves had, by their action, demonstrated that nationalization was indeed not only a dirty word but a really evil thing.

Perhaps it also explains why, according to Harold Hutchinson of the *Daily Herald*, 3,000,000 trade unionists lined up with the Tories on October 8th, 1959. Undeniably, the General Council is entitled to claim credit for that notable and third successive Tory victory.

Many Unions protested against the action of the TUC leaders in approving these appointments to the Steel Board.

It was also the subject of heated debate in the opening stages of the 1953 Congress. However, the General Council rested its case on a wordy and contradictory statement from Sir Vincent Tewson, which was printed in the General Council's Report. (1953 Congress Report, pages 254-7.)

In his statement Sir Vincent certainly tried to square the circle.

There is, stated Sir Vincent, no support to be found in anything said or done by the TUC in recent years for the view that a trade unionist agreeing to serve on a body set up to administer policy to which the TUC is opposed is, by so doing, acting in disregard of either the letter or the spirit of Congress policy.

. . . In April 1938, for example, the General Council, after considering the invitation of the then Prime Minister to discuss with him the acceleration of the rearmament programme, placed on record their

F

conviction that in dealing with any Government the Council's conduct 'must be regulated by industrial and not political considerations'.

Sir Vincent also cited the decision of the General Council to participate in the administration of the Unemployment Assistance Board, 'and it was far better for us to exert our influence to control these things rather than stand outside and have to take the consequences'.

But we find it difficult to accept Sir Vincent's argument that the representation of trade union leaders on an Unemployment Assistance Board concerned with the victims of private enterprise is the same, in principle, as the appointment of trade union leaders to a Steel Board specifically created by the Tories to demolish the nationalized character of the steel industry and hand it back to private enterprise, which provides the customers for the Unemployment Assistance Board!

There was no precedent to follow; the establishment of the Steel Board to denationalize an industry was unique. The TUC leadership had the opportunity to consult Congress before committing itself. It refrained from doing this because it knew what the answer of Congress would be.

It is idle for Sir Vincent to contend that the statements made by Sir Walter (now Lord) Citrine in 1938, which he quoted in the report in relation to public assistance or rearmament, constituted a clear indication of the intentions of Congress towards denationalization, because in 1938 nothing had been nationalized, and it was not until 1952 that the word 'denationalization' appeared in Congress Reports.

Moreover, the Bill to denationalize steel was not published until November 1952, and the September 1953 Congress was the first Congress to meet since it saw the light of day.

If Congress had been consulted on this vital issue before the leadership committed itself Sir Lincoln Evans and his two colleagues, instead of being regarded by some as traitors and by others as martyrs, would have known the wishes of Congress.

Returning to the Report, Sir Vincent went on to refer to the series of meetings of the TUC Economic Committee and the Iron and Steel Joint Sub-Committee (of which Sir Lincoln Evans was a member); a report from these Committees was submitted to the General Council in March 1953 and accepted without comment.

That was, stated Sir Vincent, until now (1953 TUC) the last time on which the General Council discussed iron and steel. However, at the June 1953 meeting of the General Council 'the following inescapable conclusions' (set out in four paragraphs) were considered:

(a) the Economic Committee were made aware as early as December 1951, of the possibility that provision would be made for trade unionists to serve on an Iron and Steel Board to be set up by the Conservative Government;

(b) through the Economic Committee and also—together with the Unions concerned, the Labour Party Executive Committee and the Parliamentary Labour Party—through their representatives on the Iron and Steel Joint Sub-Committee, the General Council were kept informed of developments as that possibility became in turn a probability, a certainty and finally a clear and specific government commitment;

(c) at no time in the course of the discussions described above did any member of the General Council or any representative of an affiliated Union or of the Labour Party Executive Committee or of the Parliamentary Labour Party, object to, or even make any adverse comment upon the proposal to appoint representative trade unionists to the Iron and Steel Board;

(d) on the contrary, by representations made directly to the Minister of Supply in association with the Unions and indirectly to the Parliamentary Labour Party through the Iron and Steel Joint Sub-Committee, General Council representatives openly and deliberately sought to make it more easily possible for representative and responsible trade unionists to accept membership of the Iron and Steel Board.

We find these four paragraphs most revealing. It seems that the TUC Economic Committee had known of the intention of the TUC to be represented on the Steel Board in 1951, even before the Steel Bill had been presented to Parliament; that the Labour Party Executive Committee and the Parliamentary Labour Party would have been as disappointed as the Tory Minister of Supply, Mr Sandys, if the TUC had declined seats on the Steel Board! We have searched the record of the debate on the Queen's Speech, when the Labour Party moved its censure motion on steel, but we can find little to support these paragraphs. Perhaps the Labour Party will throw some light on the matter.

Sir Vincent's report goes on to say that this four-paragraph statement was considered along with the letters of protest from several Unions by the General Council at their June meeting. After a full discussion the General Council adopted the following resolution by twenty votes to six, with nine people absent, six at the ILO Conference and three on trade union and other business:

'It is the long-standing and settled general policy of the TUC to insist upon the appointment of trade union representatives on all bodies set up to deal with any matter affecting the interests of workpeople.

'The Iron and Steel Board is no exception to this general rule.

'In discussions on the Iron and Steel Board that have taken place in recent months at meetings of the General Council, and of the General Council's Economic Committee, and of a joint sub-committee upon which the Unions concerned in the iron and steel industry, the Labour Party Executive Committee, and the Parliamentary Labour Party were also represented, it has always been understood and accepted that trade unionists would sit on the proposed Iron and Steel Board. The General Council must therefore reject as completely unfounded the assertion that it is incompatible with TUC policy for responsible trade unionists to serve on the Iron and Steel Board.'

Before this section of the General Council's Report could be taken, a resolution from the Boilermakers, Shipbuilders and Structural Workers had to be debated. The resolution was in the following terms:

This Congress regrets the denationalization of the iron and steel industry, and strongly deprecates the action of the members of the General Council who accepted appointments on the Tory Government's Steel Board. Should any member accept similar appointments in the future we will demand their immediate resignation from the General Council.

This resolution was seconded by the AEU and supported by the Foundry Workers and the Fire Brigades Union, while it was opposed by the Transport Salaried Staffs' Association, the National Union of Mineworkers, Sir Lincoln Evans and Sir Vincent Tewson.

It was clear that if this resolution were carried it would amount to a vote of censure on the General Council, and having regard to the method of voting at Congress it was to be expected that the possibility of its success was remote.

However, it commanded 2,877,000 votes to 4,933,000, and the General Council's report on iron and steel was thus endorsed.

CHAPTER 11

1953 ISLE OF MAN CONGRESS

TUC LEADERSHIP MAKES 'GREEN LIGHT' PROMISES

CONGRESS AGAIN, WITHOUT DISSENT, REAFFIRMS PUBLIC OWNERSHIP POLICY

But what of the mandate of the 1952 Margate Congress? Had the TUC General Council been so preoccupied assisting the Tories to bring about the denationalization of the steel industry that it had had no time to 'prepare plans for the extension of nationalization to other industries and the take-over of certain sections of the engineering and aircraft industries'?

Two weeks before the 1953 Congress opened at the Isle of Man the General Council published its usual Annual Report, and on page 277, in three short paragraphs, it revealed what had been done since the 1952 Congress.

The General Council stated:

(I) that the 1952 resolution on public ownership had been referred to the TUC Economic Committee;

(II) that the 1952 resolution on food production and farm conditions had also been referred to the Economic Committee;

(III) that the General Council had placed the services of its committees at the disposal of the Labour Party for such consultation and advice as might be necessary during the drafting of the Party's policy statement; that the Labour Party had accepted the invitation and that the representatives of the Working Parties set up by the Labour Party had attended meetings of the TUC Economic Committee in March and April. There had been a full exchange of views on the need for public ownership or control with particular reference to the following industries: shipbuilding, mining machinery, machine tools, aircraft, chemicals, civil engineering equipment and heavy electrical engineering.

The Report concluded in these terms:

The General Council's present views upon these industries are incorporated in their Interim Report on Public Ownership (also presented to the 1953 Congress) which also takes into account opinions expressed by the Labour Party representatives in the above discussions.

It is important to note that in the three paragraphs set out on page 277 of the 1953 General Council Report, and in the Interim Report on Public Ownership, there is no indication, not even the slightest hint, that the TUC leadership intended to depart from the public ownership policy which the 1952 Margate Congress had adopted.

The Interim Report itself was an excellent document. The boys in the back room had done a good job. It was a complete vindication of the industries already nationalized. It seemed, however, that the conclusions set out in the Report were not quite in keeping with the Report itself, and one delegate expressed the view from the rostrum that 'these conclusions seemed to have been drafted by a different hand'.

The TUC leadership was wise to select Mr Charles Geddes to 'lead in' and present both the appropriate paragraphs and the Interim Report to Congress.

He evidently sensed a feeling of doubt in the minds of the delegates as to whether the TUC leaders intended to shelve or pursue the public ownership policy they had adopted. His first sentence was to assure the delegates that:

This is a declaration of General Council policy and should be regarded as such, and not in the light of interpretations placed upon it.

He continued:

We are trying to set down the policy of the industrial side of the movement, and not the political side.

We are laying down here the historic future of the movement.

This report does not say 'Go back'; this report says clearly and precisely that the British trade union movement is going forward on the path of socialism by means of the expansion of social ownership.

Finally, Mr Geddes said:

I want to put this to Congress; if this report is accepted it is not a red light, as has been suggested. It is not even an amber light. It is the green light for 'go'. We accept the intention of the 1952 Congress. (1953 Congress Report, pages 383-6.)

The only other member of the TUC leadership who spoke in the debate was Mr Thomas Williamson (now Sir Thomas), who said:

I come to the rostrum to support the Interim Report of the General Council, and to say at the outset that there is nothing in the Report which opposes or obstructs the approach to public ownership . . . and that the discussions between the General Council and the Labour Party showed there was broad agreement on the question before the meeting.

Mr Williamson's statement that 'there was nothing in the Report which opposes or obstructs the approach to public ownership, and that broad agreement had been reached between the General Council and the Labour Party', without giving the delegates the slightest idea of what subjects were involved in the 'broad agreement', increased rather than allayed their apprehensions.

Many believed that the Interim Report was a calculated move to enable the TUC leadership to evade the mandate to extend public ownership, which the 1952 Congress had adopted by four and a half million votes. The delegates could not accept the plea that 'our export and financial position was too precarious to bring chemicals and engineering under public ownership', and the representatives of the National Union of Public Employees, the National Union of Railwaymen, the National Union of Shop, Distributive and Allied Workers and the Chemical Workers' Union supported the 'reference back' of the Report.

But Mr Charles Geddes carried the day. In a final speech on behalf of the TUC leadership he advised the delegates to 'wait until times are more propitious' and 'allow the General Council to go on examining the facts. Give us,' he added, 'the time and the opportunity to tell you how and when we think it should be done.'

The 1953 Congress accepted these assurances. Events, however, were to show that the TUC spokesman was quite right when he declared that the Interim Report was not a red light. It proved to be a red herring!

However, after approving the Interim Report on public ownership, Congress turned to consider a motion that had been tabled by the National Union of Mineworkers. It was in the following terms:

This Congress condemns the policy of the Tory Government in handing back to private ownership the iron and steel and the road haulage industries, and declares its continued support for the Labour

Party policy on the action it will take when again returned as the Government of this country concerning those industries that have been denationalized and for the extension of nationalization where it can be proved to be in the best interests of the nation.

Mr Arthur Horner moved this resolution. He declared that 'on account of what had occurred that afternoon' (the adoption of the Interim Report on Public Ownership) 'and as the General Council had no intention to oppose the miners' motion' he was content to move it formally.

Mr W. J. P. Webber (TSSA) seconded it, and without any further speeches it was put to Congress and carried, with no opposition.

As the TUC leadership, on its own initiative, had selected three of its number to co-operate with the Tory Government to denationalize, there was much speculation as to what were the feelings of the TUC leadership on the miners' proposal, but not a whisper came from the platform!

Whatever may have passed through the minds of the members of the General Council at that stage, they had, by withholding their opposition, avoided a repetition of the defeat they had sustained at the previous (1952 Margate) Congress.

The supporters of the policy of extending public ownership/nationalization were delighted.

At Margate in 1952 this policy, set out in comprehensive terms, was adopted by four and a half million votes, while here, at this Isle of Man Congress, the leadership had not only given the 'green light' declaration and made categorical pledges to carry out this policy, but also the miners' motion reiterating the basic principles contained in the 1952 Congress mandate had been adopted without any opposition from either the body of the hall or the platform.

In the light of the decisions of these two consecutive Congresses it was thought that as the TUC leadership was now clearly aware of the will of Congress it would apply itself with the utmost energy to the task of framing the desired social ownership programme in readiness for the General Election.

Subsequent events were to show how these hopes were shattered and to what extent the democratic decisions of Congress were to be disregarded and the membership deceived.

CHAPTER 12

1954 BRIGHTON CONGRESS

AGAIN REAFFIRMS PUBLIC OWNERSHIP POLICY

BUT TUC LEADERS HAVE OTHER IDEAS
ABOUT IT

At the 1953 Isle of Man Congress the late Mr Arthur Deakin, General Secretary of the Transport and General Workers' Union, the biggest block vote holder in Congress, sat on the platform while the Interim Report on public ownership was debated and was able to note that not only Congress but also his own delegation voted unanimously for it.

Whether he personally disliked the Report or not, as a member of the TUC General Council, if there is anything at all in collective responsibility, he was committed to it, and yet three weeks later, at the Margate Labour Party Conference which opened on September 28, 1953, when he intervened in the debate on the draft policy statement 'Challenge to Britain', he completely disregarded not only the terms of the Interim Report on public ownership but also many other policy decisions of Congress.

Referring to the 'Plan for Engineering', a publication of the engineering unions which the TUC General Council had undertaken to consider in framing its public ownership programme, Mr Deakin, in the presence of the representatives of the national and world press, made this amazing statement:

The so-called Plan is just a mumbo-jumbo of meaningless words and phrases (Cries of 'Nonsense'.) I would go further in response to that challenge and say it is the worst abortion ever conceived in the mind of man . . . There are two tests to apply. First, is the industry sufficiently efficient to do the nation's work? The engineering industry, whatever its critics may say, has done a fine job of work; it has shaped up to its responsibilities, it has filled the export markets with its goods that are so necessary to our survival in a very satisfactory manner and it ought to be dealt with in such a way that the efficiency is maintained and developed.

... If you want to maintain that do not drive us into the position of falling out and breaking with the Party on such an issue as this. (Labour Party Report 1953, pages 124-5.)

This dictate from Mr Deakin, in defiance of TUC decisions, with its remarkable boost of private enterprise and the threat that he would bust up the Party if his wishes were ignored, led to general uproar, and those who attended the conference are unlikely to forget it.

This was certainly a strange way for a member of the TUC leadership to carry out the public ownership policy which less than a month earlier the Isle of Man Congress had unanimously adopted! The Tories were delighted. Arthur Deakin had provided them with their best curtain raiser for the (May) 1955 General Election.

After Mr Deakin's outburst at the Margate Labour Party Conference the next TUC Congress opened at Brighton in September 1954. When the delegates assembled it was expected that Mr Deakin would either attempt to justify his damaging statements or retract them and offer his resignation from the General Council. He did neither. In the TUC set-up the big fellows are not subject to these requirements. They are laws unto themselves.

This incident, however, reinforces the conviction that the present TUC organization will never be able to honour its own pledges nor implement its own decisions in respect of either public ownership policy or trade union reform, because the competitive, conflicting and anti-social interests within it are too powerful to allow it.

Mr Deakin was a man of great personal integrity, but he was also the leader of a 'general' type of union. His violent opposition to the public ownership of but a few sections of the engineering industry is understandable because, in a publicly owned and efficiently run industry, the general type of union has no place and would soon decline and disappear.

But what was the effect of Mr Deakin's conduct on the General Council and the TUC Economic Committee? Had it discouraged or incited interest in the implementation of the Interim Report on public ownership?

In the General Council's Report submitted to the 1954 Brighton Congress there was little evidence to show that 'the British trade union movement is going forward on the path of *socialism by means of public ownership'*, as the TUC leader, Mr Geddes, prophesied at the Isle of Man a year ago.

In this Report the TUC leadership gave an account of the 'further action' it had taken in respect of the Interim Report on public ownership. It was difficult for the delegates to determine either the character or the extent of this 'further action', because all the Report revealed to them was expressed in the following paragraph:

That at the October meeting of the TUC Economic Committee it had considered further action to be taken after the approval by Congress of the Interim Report on public ownership. They also took into account the 1953 TUC resolution expressing support for the renationalization of road haulage and iron and steel, and for the extension of nationalization to other industries, and that the Committee noted that this resolution accorded with the Interim Report. (1954 Congress Report, pages 285-6.)

In subsequent paragraphs, however, various explanations for certain delays were given.

As regards coal mining, further consideration was deferred until the National Union of Mineworkers had reached definite conclusions about the financial structure of the industry. Nothing further had been heard from the NUM on this subject.

The General Council's discussions with the Confederation of Shipbuilding and Engineering Unions had also not gone smoothly, and the Deakin incident had brought the General Council's examination of the engineering industry to a standstill. The Report states:

On October 19th a letter was sent to the Confederation to which no direct reply was received. On October 26th, however, the Confederation wrote to the General Council complaining about remarks made by Mr Deakin at the Labour Party Conference at Margate in September referring to the 'Plan for Engineering'. The Confederation asked for a statement of the General Council's views on the 'Plan' in the light of these remarks. The General Council replied to the Confederation on November 27th that their attitude towards the 'Plan for Engineering' remained as set out in the Interim Report, i.e. that they were willing to discuss the various proposals of the 'Plan' with representatives of the Confederation during the present Congress year. As to the statement by Mr Deakin, the General Council had neither the authority nor the desire to attempt to question the right of any organization affiliated to the Labour Party to appoint and instruct its delegates to the Party Conference.

No further communication had been received from the Confederation. Under the circumstances the General Council have thought it impracticable to proceed with their examination of the engineering industry.

The General Council's admission that it had 'neither the authority nor the desire' to reprimand Mr Deakin for flagrantly disregarding, at the Labour Party Conference, the decisions of the TUC General Council (of which he was a member) and those of Congress itself, shows what a strange outfit the TUC really is. If a member of the Cabinet, of any Party, subscribed to a decision inside the Cabinet but denounced it outside, he would soon know his fate! Mr Deakin, however, for his act of irresponsibility, was able to cock a snook at his complainants and also have the satisfaction of preventing the General Council from 'proceeding with the examination of the engineering industry'.

After disposing of the Deakin affair, the General Council in its Report went on to describe what further action had been taken on the Interim Report on public ownership:

The TUC Economic Committee had decided to carry out a review of the working of the Development Councils.

The TUC Economic Committee decided to concentrate first on marketing and distribution policy.

The TUC Economic Committee agreed to an inquiry into private investing institutions and that further attention would be given to the work of the Monopolies Commission. (1954 Brighton Report, pages 286-7.)

This vague report conveyed the impression that everything would be taken care of—but not just yet!

But before the 1954 Brighton Congress concluded, the interest of the delegates in the extension of public ownership was further demonstrated.

A composite motion on 'Public Ownership' was tabled in the names of the ETU, AUBTW, AEU, ASLE & F and the Chemical Workers' Union.

The composite motion by these five important Unions was in the following terms:

This Congress records its profound conviction that the extension of public ownership to decisive sections of the national economy is a vital prerequisite for the achievement of an ordered, efficient and progressive economy capable of maintaining and improving the living standards of the people. Accordingly, Congress confirms ownership of the basic industries, which include certain sections of the chemical and engineering industries.

Congress also realizes that the building and civil engineering industries, together with the building materials industry, have a bad record of restrictive practices. As a step towards ending the present chaotic and costly control by private enterprise, Congress approves the policy outlined in 'Challenge to Britain' for a National Building Corporation responsible for the development of contracts by direct labour. Congress further believes that the co-operative technique of voluntary common ownership should be accepted as an important element in the structure of society both now and for the future. (1954 Brighton Congress Report, page 467.)

There were no faint hearts or doubtful starters among the five Unions promoting this composite, and instead of there being the usual differences of principle or of emphasis they all subscribed to a single composite motion.

In the absence of disagreement the delegates would not be confused by having more than one composite motion before them at the same time.

It is easy for the composite technique (described in another part of the book) to be exploited by the leadership when there is more than one composite to be debated, but when there is only one it means a single issue of 'for' or 'against' the one motion, and the strength of the argument is all the more apparent.

At the same time, however, when agreement is reached by the representatives of several differently situated Unions on a composite motion, it is to be expected that it will have rather a wide coverage.

Be that as it may, the fact that five important Unions recorded the conviction of their members that they regarded 'the extension of public ownership . . . as a vital prerequisite for the achievement of an ordered, efficient and progressive economy, capable of maintaining and improving the living standards of the people', was of great significance, and it showed the mental attitude of trade unionists to the most vital economic and political issue of the day.

When Mr Foulkes (ETU) moved the motion the atmosphere

was charged with expectation. In the light of what had happened at Margate in 1952 and at the Isle of Man in 1953, would the Brighton Congress in 1954 make it a triple achievement for the policy of public ownership?

Mr G. H. Lowthian (AUBTW) seconded the composite motion. He and Foulkes were the only two speakers from the floor, because immediately Mr Lowthian concluded the President asked Congress whether the vote could then be taken.

Apparently the leadership thought discretion to be the better part of valour, as its spokesman made it known that the General Council did not intend to oppose the composite.

After a short statement from Mr W. L. Heywood, Chairman of the TUC's Economic Committee, the composite motion was put to Congress and carried without opposition.

Contrary to one's fears, it was hoped that in the General Council's next Report, which will be presented to Congress at Southport in September 1955, it will be able to disclose to the delegates the more positive steps it has taken to carry out the pledges it made at the Isle of Man and present the outline of the public ownership programme in accordance with the 1952 decision and the 1953 Interim Report.

CHAPTER 13

LABOUR SUSTAINS ITS SECOND GENERAL ELECTION DEFEAT

1955 SOUTHPORT CONGRESS REAFFIRMS ITS FAITH IN PUBLIC OWNERSHIP

In the May 1955 General Election Labour sustained its second defeat. The results showed that over a period of ten years from 1945 to 1955 Labour's percentage of the total poll had declined from 48·8% to 46·3%, while the Tories had increased their portion from 39% to 49·8%.

Such depressing results showed the need for the TUC to devise an industrial programme related to the needs of the times and the desires of its 8,176,252 members. Unless it did so further defeats would be inevitable.

The movement had already paid a heavy price for the TUC's abject failure to design an effective industrial programme. Would it now make amends, end its procrastinating tactics and hasten to carry out the instructions of Congress?

When the Southport Congress opened in September 1955 it was hoped that the TUC leadership would be able to reveal what progress it had made in preparing the public ownership programme in accordance with the mandate of the 1952 Margate Congress.

As three years had passed since that Congress it was not unreasonable to expect the TUC leaders to give delegates an idea of their plans, if only in broad outline.

It is true that the leadership had presented an 'Interim Report' to the Isle of Man Congress which followed the 1952 Margate Congress, but that 'Interim Report' only increased our expectancy. On that occasion did not Mr C. Geddes, on behalf of the leadership, make his notable 'green light' speech, that was loaded with pledges, in order to assure the doubting delegates that the TUC leaders would faithfully carry out the 1952 Congress decision?

Surely, if the TUC leaders were in earnest and intended to

carry out that decision, there should be, after three whole years of gestation, some visible signs of their labours.

But were they in earnest? Or had it dawned upon them that, having regard to the present TUC set-up and the prevailing trade union disorder, they were in fact incapable of devising any effective public ownership programme?

If they were in earnest but realized that organizational defects prevented them from carrying out this Congress mandate, could it be expected that these TUC leaders, in the light of their record, would blurt out the truth that until the TUC set-up was radically altered and a more rational method of trade union organization established there was no hope of designing a programme for the extension of public ownership?

But there are no signs that the TUC leadership will, of its own volition, ever take such a step. It is more likely that it will continue to keep up its present policy of make-believe, and hope that by delay and skilful manoeuvre it will get through as it has on so many occasions in the past.

While awaiting the revelation at Southport many delegates were assailed by doubts and suspicions. Their confidence in the TUC leadership had been seriously shaken.

The pledge to 'work amicably' with the Tory Government; the appointment of three trade union leaders to sit on the Steel Board to help the denationalization of the nationalized steel industry; the action of Mr Arthur Deakin (the most powerful member of the TUC leadership) at the 1953 Labour Party Conference in flouting the public ownership mandate of the Trades Union Congress held three weeks earlier and his threat to withdraw his Union from Labour Party affiliation if any attempt were made to bring the engineering industry or any part of it into public ownership, were incidents fresh in the minds of the delegates, who were not inspired by them.

But perhaps these were mere errors of judgment or tactical indiscretions, and now at this 1955 Southport Congress the TUC leadership would show that instead of side-tracking the 1952, 1953 and 1954 public ownership decisions of Congress it would honour them and carry them out.

This hope was not realized. All the TUC leaders had to reveal was expressed in seventeen lines in their Report to Congress, which stated:

Public Ownership

It was reported last year that because of the failure of the Confederation of Shipbuilding and Engineering Unions to reply to their invitation to discuss further the proposals in the 'Plan for Engineering', the General Council had had to defer their examination of the engineering industry.

Since no communication had been received from the Confederation by March of this year, the General Council gave preliminary consideration to the problems facing certain sections of the engineering industry and approved documents analyzing these problems, and the relevance of various proposals for public ownership or control to their solution, as a basis for discussion with the Confederation. On March 23rd a further letter was addressed to the Confederation asking if they were yet ready to resume discussions. On April 26th the Confederation replied that they were ready to resume discussions with representatives of the General Council. Copies of the documents which had been prepared were therefore sent to the Confederation for their comments, and when these are received arrangements will be made for meetings between the Confederation's representatives and the appropriate Committee of the General Council to discuss them. (1955 Southport Congress Report, page 274.)

That, and that alone, was the extent of the leadership's endeavours to carry out the mandate of the 1952 Congress to provide a comprehensive public ownership programme!

It was apparent that the TUC leadership, by using the Confederation as a sort of alibi, was preparing the way to disregard the four and a half million decision of Margate and its own pledges made a year later at the Isle of Man Congress.

It was too much to expect that Congress would remain silent and allow this unsatisfactory seventeen-line report of the leadership to pass without protest. A delegate of the National Union of Public Employees availed himself of the right to move the 'reference back' of this Report, and what happened is shown in the following statement extracted from the official Report (Southport Congress Report 1955, pages 416-7):

Public Ownership

The National Union of Public Employees' representative said: I want to move the reference back of paragraph 321. At Margate in 1952, by over four and a half million votes, Congress instructed the General Council to formulate proposals for the extension of social ownership in the engineering and other industries. At the 1953 Con-

G

gress the General Council presented an interim report which Mr Geddes himself introduced in an extremely eloquent speech after which the report was adopted. I do not suggest that Mr Geddes used his eloquence to mislead the delegates. I have too high an opinion of him to make that suggestion. But the fact remains that it is difficult to square the statements and promises then made with this dreary paragraph in the Report.

In 1953 we were sold a pup. We were then told that in the interim report we were laying down the historic future of this movement; that it would fill the vacuum between capitalism and communism; that it was not a cry to halt but pointed a clear road forward; that it was not a red light, not even an amber light, but it was green for go. That is what we were told in 1953.

That was two years ago. If the delegates can find any signs of this historic future, or any sign of the green light in this part of the Report they must be as colour blind as the General Council. I ask you: do the promises in 1953 match this pathetic performance? Last year the General Council sought to excuse their failure because they had had no reply to a letter to the Confederation of Shipbuilding and Engineering Unions. This year the General Council have done nothing because they are waiting for a reply to a letter to the Confederation. I think it is a most wretched alibi.

Moreover, the 1952 mandate did not commit the Council either to adopting or rejecting the 'Plan for Engineering'. It simply said that due regard should be paid to it, which left the Council free to bring up their own proposals for the extension of social ownership in the engineering industry. The General Council have not done this. They have defaulted on their mandate. They have made no attempt to do it. We are back precisely where we started in 1952.

Three valuable years have passed since the Margate Congress instructed the General Council to draw up a social ownership programme. Yet not a single blueprint, not even a rough outline has appeared. Indeed, all reference to the interim report has been dropped from the Report presented to Congress. The General Council, I presume, are hoping that the delegates have forgotten all about it and the statements made in 1953. I say we shall pay dearly for this dismal failure. We lost the last General Election in my view because we did not have a real industrial programme, and we shall deserve to lose the next if steps are not taken to implement the decision reached at Margate three years ago.

I ask Congress, therefore, to realize the urgency of this matter and press upon the General Council their obligation to carry out the 1952 mandate, and I hope Congress will agree to support the reference back which I move.

Mr W. L. Heywood (General Council), speaking in support of the General Council, said:

NUPE's representative has criticized the General Council for their failure, as he alleges, to go ahead with the plans for economic and industrial reconstruction, the plans for social ownership. But he must know as well as anybody in this room the reasons for the delay there has been. NUPE's representative, indeed, referred to the differences between the General Council and in particular some members of the General Council and the AEU and the Confederation of Shipbuilding and Engineering Unions. It is perfectly well known that a good deal of the delay has been the consequence of the unwillingness of the AEU and the Confederation to join with the General Council in further consideration of what ought to be done in that section of British industry. Those differences have been resolved, and the General Council therefore submitted months ago to the Confederation documents setting out the views of the General Council on proposals for different sections of the engineering industry.

Congress must remember that 'the engineering industry' is in a sense a misleading term. The engineering trade is a collection of several different industries, and it is a very large task, and a very important one, from the point of view of the millions of workers employed in it, that the job should be properly done. I do not think it is fair that complaint should be made that a considerable time is being taken over this matter. I do not complain at the delay there has been. Indeed, I do not think delay is the right word. I do not complain of the time that has elapsed in the consideration by the Confederation and the unions in the engineering trade of the proposals put forward by the General Council. I think it is desirable that they should consider carefully the implications of the documents that have been put up, and I think NUPE's representative is unjustified in speaking so strongly and with such little regard for the trend of events as he has spoken this morning.

The General Council have continuously looked at this matter. There has never been a meeting of the Economic Committee for a considerable time past when documents and proposals of one kind or another on the broad aspects of social ownership and of its application to the individual industries have not been before the Economic Committee. Therefore there has been no undue delay having regard to all the circumstances. Some of the delay is unfortunate, some of it is healthy because it means that matters are being carefully and accurately considered, and I have no hesitation whatever in asking Congress to reject the reference back.

Congress, no matter how displeased it may be, is always reluctant to carry a 'reference back' motion because it amounts to a vote of censure against the General Council. The reluctance of Congress and the voting system usually combine to defeat such a motion, as it did on this occasion.

But did this mean a different attitude on the part of Congress to the issue of public ownership? It certainly did not.

This same 1955 Congress, after disposing of the 'reference back', proceeded to consider for the fourth consecutive year a composite motion calling for the nationalization of the basic industries. It was moved by the AEU, seconded by the Amalgamated Union of Foundry Workers and supported by the Chemical Workers' Union.

However, Mr J. Campbell (General Council) intervened and intimated that while the General Council was in agreement with the underlying principles of the motion he asked that it be remitted to the General Council. (Southport 1955 Congress Report, pages 417-20.)

This was agreed to.

No opposition whatever was expressed against this further motion supporting the nationalization of our basic industries, and it could be said that each year since 1952 Congress had consistently supported the principles of public ownership, in spite of the fact that so far the General Council had done so little about it.

CHAPTER 14

1956 BRIGHTON CONGRESS

TUC LEADERSHIP FURTHER REPORT ON PUBLIC OWNERSHIP

NO HINT YET OF POLICY SWITCH

It cannot be said that Labour lost the 1955 General Election because our industrial programme was either ineffective or unsuitable, because on that occasion we presented to the electors no industrial programme at all.

Now that this second consecutive defeat was so fresh in the minds of the TUC leaders surely they would now realize that an attractive and realistic industrial programme is essential to a Labour victory and that they must, straight away, get down to the job of devising such an industrial programme in readiness for the time when the Tories made their next appeal to the country.

In this expectation we eagerly awaited the TUC General Council's Report to the 1956 Brighton Congress. When this Report did appear in the hands of the delegates its contents hardly convinced them that that was what the leadership now intended to do. It was, however, encouraging to note from the Report that the TUC had reached agreement with the Confederation of Shipbuilding and Engineering Unions on the subject of the public ownership of the machine tools industry. In the light of the remarks of the late Mr Arthur Deakin at the 1953 Labour Party Margate Conference the agreement was particularly welcome.

There was little else to cause the delegates to believe that the TUC leadership was straining at the leash to fulfil the public ownership mandates of Congress. Nevertheless, there was no cause to doubt the intention of the leadership, because on page 296 of the 1956 Brighton Report it made it clear that it was still pursuing the subject of public ownership in accordance with the principles laid down in the 1944 Report on Post-War Reconstruction and those set out in the 1953 Interim Report on Public Ownership. We welcomed these assurances, although we did not know at the time that they were to be so quickly disregarded. But let us defer comment on these assurances until a later stage. Here, let us relate from page 296 of the 1956 Report the further views of the leadership. The leadership of the General Council advised the delegates that:

... they would be resuming discussions with the Confederation of Shipbuilding and Engineering Unions on the engineering industry, and that their proposals for the chemical industry had been set out in the 'Report on Public Ownership' which was endorsed by the 1953 Congress.

... in the case of the building and building materials industries, the General Council, in respect of the 1955 composite, decided to write the promoting unions asking for their views on the relevant sections of the composite. A number of unions had replied and these replies would be taken into account in the preparation of a detailed study of these industries by the General Council.

. as reported last year, documents on certain sections of the engineering industry had been sent to the Confederation of Shipbuilding and Engineering Unions ... A letter had been received from the Confederation in July indicating their acceptance of the TUC document dealing with the machine tools industry.

Even if, according to the 1956 Report of the General Council's preparations for the desired public ownership programme, they were no farther advanced now than they were when the Interim Report on public ownership was submitted to the 1953 Isle of Man Congress, when Mr Geddes (General Council) made his famous 'green light' speech, it was some consolation to note that the hearts of the TUC leaders and those of the Confederation were now beating in unison!

Now, surely, nothing could prevent the formulation of the desired industrial programme, based on public ownership, which alone can retrieve our trade union and political fortunes and best serve the nation's needs.

But we were unaware of the surprises that lay ahead.

CHAPTER 15

1957 BLACKPOOL CONGRESS

THE POLICY SWITCH BEGINS

'IT IS ONLY AN ADJUNCT!'

At each Congress from 1952 to 1957 resolutions demanding the extension of public ownership had been carried. The first resolution in 1952 had been carried by four and a half million votes, while in the subsequent Congresses similar resolutions commanded unanimity, there being no opposition from either the platform or the floor.

At this 1957 Congress we were to learn from the TUC General Council what progress the TUC leadership had made in carrying out the mandates on public ownership since its report a year ago.

ENGINEERING INDUSTRIES

This up-to-date statement of the General Council (Blackpool 1957 Congress Report, pages 299-300) revealed that:

the Confederation of Shipbuilding and Engineering Unions had written to the General Council in *September* 1956 saying that they were ready to resume discussions and enclosing a resolution adopted at their Annual Conference asking the TUC and the Labour Party to prepare a plan for the nationalization of appropriate sections of the engineering and shipbuilding industries.

... when the Economic Committee considered this letter it readily agreed to meet the Confederation's representatives. The Economic Committee also decided to send the Confederation documents bringing up to date the information contained in documents on the shipbuilding and marine engineering, machine tools, railway locomotives and railway rolling stock industries, which had some time previously been sent to the Confederation.

The General Council's Report then refers to a meeting with the Confederation back in November 1956. It appears from this reference that certain statements from the Confederation had been lost in the post. However, the Confederation's representatives had outlined their criticism of certain aspects of some of the documents submitted by the General Council, but it was agreed that the meeting had clarified the position and the Confederation's representatives undertook to submit further observations.

MACHINE TOOLS INDUSTRY

In its short, two-paragraph report on machine tools, the General Council revealed that there was much unanimity between the General Council and the Confederation, as the report declares that:

> After it had received and examined the Confederation's comments (on the machine tools industry) the TUC Economic Committee noted that the Confederation's views were broadly similar to those which had been set out in the TUC's own account. The General Council had, therefore, informed the Confederation that in their view it was not necessary to hold a special meeting on the machine tools industry, but that points which either side wished to discuss might well be raised at a subsequent meeting on other industries.

AIRCRAFT INDUSTRY

The previous optimistic note was continued in a single paragraph on the aircraft industry. It declared:

> The Economic Committee had in the meantime been examining the structure and problems of the aircraft industry. In April (1956) it forwarded to the Confederation a document examining the case for public ownership control over the industry, with the suggestion that it should be dealt with in the same way as previous documents.

The reader is invited to note very carefully these extracts from the General Council Report which was circulated to the affiliated Unions just a fortnight before Congress assembled at Blackpool on September 2, 1957.

He is also invited to note that the Report reveals that in September 1956 the Confederation had written the General Council asking that, in the light of the Confederation's Annual Conference, a plan for the nationalization of appropriate sections of the engineering and shipbuilding industries be prepared, which request was also in line with Congress decisions previously taken.

Note too that in respect of the machine tools industry the views of the TUC Economic Committee and the Confederation were 'broadly similar', and any outstanding points could be considered when discussing other industries.

Again, the TUC Economic Committee had been closely examining the structure and problems of the aircraft industry, and in April 1956 it had forwarded documents to the Confederation, inviting their observations.

These meetings referred to above, and the dates on which they were held, seem to have a special significance in the light of the section which follows. It is:

Public Ownership of Industry—
Labour Party Study Group

In February (1957) the Study Group of the Labour Party National Executive Committee, which had been considering future policy on the ownership of industry, indicated that they would welcome an exchange of views with the General Council on a preliminary draft of the statement which they were preparing. The TUC Economic Committee met the Study Group on March 21st (1957) for an exchange of views. In May 1957 the Economic Committee considered a later draft of the Labour Party statement and its views on it were conveyed to the Study Group. The Labour Party statement was published in July 1957. (1957 Blackpool Congress Report, page 300.)

This apparently innocuous statement was the first occasion that Congress was advised that the TUC Economic Committee had discussed with the Party Study Group a preliminary draft of a policy statement which the latter were preparing. There was nothing strange in that; it gave not the slightest hint that the TUC even contemplated throwing overboard its own public ownership policy which year after year Congress, by huge votes, had instructed the TUC leadership to pursue.

Could the 1957 Congress imagine that while the General Council was in discussion with the Confederation of Shipbuilding and Engineering Unions' representatives on a public ownership programme, the representatives of the TUC Economic Committee, without any mandate, were acquiescing in or perhaps pursuing a contrary policy with the Labour Party Study Group?

Congress was unaware of what was going on. Section 380 (page 300) of the 1957 General Council Report simply told Congress that the TUC Economic Committee had met the Study Group and had an exchange of views, and that the Committee had, in May 1957, considered a later draft of the proposed

Labour Party statement, on which the TUC Economic Committee had submitted its views to the Study Group, without even disclosing to the affiliated Unions what those views were.

Beyond these bald facts the 1957 Congress had no information. What the TUC Economic Committee told the Labour Party Study Group and what the Study Group told the Economic Committee only the members of these two bodies know, and that secrecy was maintained until July 1957, when the Labour Party published *Industry and Society*.

'INDUSTRY AND SOCIETY'

When copies of the Labour Party's policy statement called *Industry and Society* were received it was noted with great astonishment that beyond providing for the renationalization of steel and road haulage the statement completely ignored the decisions of the TUC in respect of further public ownership.

The decision of the 1952 Margate Congress, the Interim Report on Public Ownership adopted by the 1953 Isle of Man Congress and all the subsequent decisions (approved without any opposition vote), right up to 1957, commanded not a single reference and were completely disregarded.

For five and more years countless hours had been devoted by the TUC delegates to the preparation of public ownership motions, to compositing and debating them. Under the direction of the General Council the TUC research staff had spent weeks, months and years on the preparation of documents, and a great deal of time and attention had also been expended by the Confederation for the purpose of furthering the public ownership mandates of Congress.

And all this, so it seemed, was now just so much waste. The extension of public ownership, which is a fundamental policy of Congress, *Industry and Society* proposed to scrap, and, without consulting Congress, to substitute a policy of investing in selected capitalist concerns.

It was an astonishing thing that this statement should be issued as a public document without the Congress delegates having a chance to consider it, and for this the TUC General Council carries a heavy responsibility.

Had the TUC leaders been converted to the 'investment policy', or had they vigorously opposed it and supported the traditional policy of public ownership in accordance with the mandates of Congress?

We don't know the answer to this question because the brief statement set out on page 300 of the Report doesn't give a clue to what the TUC leadership said to the Labour Party Study Group or what the Study Group said to the TUC leadership. We are still in the dark.

And why was it that *Industry and Society* was published but a few days after the closing date for the submission of motions to the 1957 TUC? Was it just a coincidence, or was it intentional in order to prevent the 1957 Blackpool Congress from considering it?

These are pertinent and proper questions. If it was just an accident that *Industry and Society* appeared when it was too late to submit resolutions on it to the 1957 Congress, the TUC General Council still had nearly two months to prepare and publish its own report to Congress.

It could have told us what had been its attitude to the Labour Party Study Group and whether it agreed to scrap its own Congress policy in favour of the new investment policy. It could have set out a précis of *Industry and Society* that would have enabled any delegate to challenge any aspect of the statement by moving the 'reference back'.

But even this usual right could not be exercised because section 380 on page 300, consisting of but four sentences, simply confined itself to telling Congress that the TUC Economic Committee had met the Labour Party Study Group.

Did the TUC leadership deliberately exclude from its Report all reference to the statement *Industry and Society* in order to prevent any delegate from raising the matter, thus avoiding the possibility that Congress might upset the relations of members of the TUC Economic Committee with members of the Labour Party Study Group?

Whether this was intended or not, it was fortunate that three Unions, NUPE, the AUBTW and the CEU, had tabled motions on aspects of public ownership for the 1957 Congress before *Industry and Society* was published, and that fact enabled them to refer to the Labour Party document without being ruled out of order. These Unions agreed to composite their three motions in the following terms:

This Congress notes that it has not yet been possible for the General Council to carry out the mandate of the 1952 Margate Congress and the pledges given to the 1953 Congress in respect of social ownership.

Congress therefore instructs the General Council to work for the implementation of such policy in order that the trade union movement can determine the part it is to play, in conjunction with the political wing of the movement, in shaping Labour's next General Election programme.

The representative of the National Union of Public Employees moved this composite motion. He said (1957 Blackpool Congress Report, page 457):

The 1952 Congress, by four and a half million votes, declared its faith in public ownership and mandated the General Council to formulate plans for its extension to other industries and services. At the 1953 Congress it will be remembered the General Council presented an interim report and made very definite pledges that it would prepare plans, and once again it reaffirmed its faith in public ownership. The interim report, said the General Council member who had introduced it, was the green light for 'go', and it was designed to fill the vacuum between capitalism and socialism.

That was four years ago, and the old bus is still standing at the traffic lights. I know the General Council have had their difficulties, but they had a mandate to do a job and they should have done it. I believe that had it been done sooner the present difficulty over Party policy would not have arisen. Anyway, the politicians seem to have taken advantage of our dilatoriness, because according to interpretation they now propose to fill Charlie Geddes' famous vacuum with something like Moral Re-Armament. They believe, again according to certain interpretations, that our emancipation can be achieved through the board room of the giant companies and the love and kindness of disinterested company directors and the benevolent and public-spirited shareholders.

There is, however, a very serious aspect to all this. It shows, on paper at least, that there is a serious difference on the issue of public ownership between the declared policy of Congress and the Party leaders, which indeed is not a very propitious beginning for the forthcoming General Election campaign. This difference must not be allowed to develop into a conflict, and it should be quickly resolved, preferably before and not after the Party Conference. It may well cost us the General Election if it is not. But to have allowed such a situation to be created at all seems to show a lamentable lack of statesmanship. Were there not any joint consultations? Were the programme drafters unaware of Congress declarations? Were they unaware, for instance, of our decision in relation to the water industry? Or were they made aware of these declarations and decisions and decided to ignore them? If that be so, it would be most regrettable indeed. This Congress is jealous of its right to shape industrial policy, and not to have one imposed upon it. Congress is a partner—a senior partner—and not a poor relation.

Public ownership is our main socialist armament, and while it may be assisted by other weapons, financial and otherwise, it should not be relegated and wrapped up in moth balls; it should remain in Labour's front line. We believe that without public ownership an equitable, secure and planned economy is impossible. If that belief is respected I believe it is possible to reach common ground with the Party and to preserve our essential unity.

Our industrial situation makes it imperative not to restrict but to extend public ownership in accordance with our 1952 Congress decision and the 1953 Interim Report. Industrial unrest is increasing; it may well get out of hand. The task of trade union negotiators is becoming ever more difficult. Under private enterprise the workers cannot share the results of increased productivity nor receive a fair share of the overall prosperity of the industry in which they are employed. Wages—the engineering dispute showed this—are now based, not on the richest companies, but on the poorest and least efficient; that is how capital gains are accumulated. Public ownership is the only means of bringing about industrial integration that will enable the workers to share in the overall prosperity of the industry and at the same time provide them with real incentives. Public ownership is no longer a socialist fantasy; public ownership is a real urgent national necessity.

This motion, in addition to being a reaffirmation, provides the opportunity for the General Council, with the authority of Congress, which I think is so important, to have discussions with the Party in the hope that policy differences will be cleared up and that we shall face the Tories in the coming election as a united movement and not as a divided one.

Mr G. H. Lowthian (AUBTW) seconded the motion, and Messrs E. Patterson (CEU) and R. J. Gunter (TSSA) supported.

Before the vote was taken Mr W. L. Heywood made the following statement on behalf of the General Council:

The General Council find nothing to object to in the general terms of the motion before you, but, in view of the present situation they consider it desirable that a statement should be made from the platform. As the motion refers to the pledges given some years ago, and as NUPE's representative was at pains to expand the criticism which he has made from time to time on that aspect of the matter, I think it is incumbent on me, first of all, to make some reference to that part of the motion.

The presentation of the Interim Report on Public Ownership to the 1953 Congress was, in my submission, a discharge of our commitments up to that date. In that document, which was accepted by Congress, we undertook to consider in detail the position of certain key industries in the country and work in conjunction with the unions concerned in deciding policy and making recommendations about those sections of industry. An immense amount of work has been done in this field, mainly in the engineering industry but by no means confined to the engineering industry. The engineering industry is a collection of trades, and it requires to be approached sectionally, if we are to get anywhere through the labyrinth which the engineering industry now is, as it sprawls across the economic activity of the country. We have submitted from time to time most detailed documents to the Confederation of Shipbuilding and Engineering Unions on sections of the engineering trade. It is true that there has been some delay, but it has not at all been the fault of the General Council. Such time consumption is inevitable if federations are adequately to consider the most detailed examination of trades in which they have a special interest and of which they have a particular knowledge.

The present position between the General Council and the Confederation is that in one section of the engineering trades we have reached general agreement, and for that reason we are surprised to see a motion on the machine tools industry.

At the moment there are four other documents in the possession of the Confederation and we are awaiting their comments. The last of them, on the aircraft industry, I make bold to say—and I am only repeating what I said as chairman of the committee when the document was adopted for communication to the Confederation—is one of the best documents and best examinations of an industry that has ever been turned out in this country in its detail and its grasp of what is essential.

Mr Lowthian has reminded the Congress that only three weeks ago there were discussions between the building trade unions and the Economic Committee on the proposals which are under examination for building and there is a good deal of other work—agricultural marketing, investment policy, coal distribution, public control of monopolies, and so on. All that work is going on and the unions concerned in particular aspects have been kept informed and have, from time to time, communicated their views to the General Council. We regard the commitment as a continuing one and it will go on, and no doubt eventually NUPE's representative will be convinced that something useful has been achieved.

The motion asks us to work in conjunction with the political wing of the Labour Movement. We have done that in these matters. Wherever there have been points of political significance that required consultation, those consultations have taken place. But, in addition to that, representatives of the Labour Party Executive sit monthly with the Economic Committee of the General Council, and contact is maintained in that way.

That brings me to the point that has excited so much comment this week, namely, the new policy document of the Labour Party. This is not the Labour Party Conference and the Labour Party Conference is entitled to make its own decisions about Labour Party policy. I should object if the Labour Party Conference sought to usurp the rights of the Trades Union Congress, and we must not make the contrary mistake here in Blackpool this week. But the critics, those who have doubt, should look at the Party document and see what the Party document does in fact say about nationalization. It says on page 57 that 'in the case of steel and long distance road haulage, the case for public ownership remains as strong as ever. We shall, accordingly, restore public ownership in these industries. Beyond that, we reserve the right to extend public ownership in any industry or part of industry which, after thorough inquiry, is found to be seriously failing the nation.'

The Labour Party, therefore, in its own document, has given assurances that it will continue, where necessary, to use the instrument of complete nationalization.

If I may take credit for this on behalf of the General Council, a member of the Labour Party Executive, within the last two or three weeks, has expressed the view in the country that a certain section of the engineering industry was soon to be taken into public ownership if a Labour Government was returned, and that is the section of the engineering industry about which we have reached agreement broadly with the Confederation. It is not mere speculation to say that the work that the Congress has done in that field has largely influenced statements of that kind.

On the General Council we do not regard the Labour Party document as being irreconcilable with the general programme of public ownership to which the Congress is committed. We regard it as an adjunct. I am sure that is what Mr Gunter was speaking about in his admirable speech a few moments ago, that this is a necessary adjunct to the authority of the Party to nationalize whole industries as and when the occasion requires and makes desirable.

But I think I am entitled to remind NUPE's representative of something else. In 1953 at Douglas I spoke after him in the public ownership discussion, and it is on record that I then pointed out to him that if there were to be two concurrent examinations of the problems of public ownership, one conducted by the TUC and another by the Labour Party, one organization with industrial interests and the other having to watch electoral possibilities, there would necessarily and inevitably be differences of emphasis and timing. We ought not to complain about that. The more work done, the more investigation there is, the more consideration, the better it will be.

Finally, in fairness to the Labour Party, let me dispel the idea of the minds of mischief makers outside that the unity in the Labour Party Executive Committee on their proposals is shadow boxing, face saving or illusory. When we met the Labour Party Committee on this subject there was complete unanimity on their side. Mr Aneurin Bevan spoke enthusiastically and strongly in support of the policy document. He need not have done so; he was not the spokesman of the Party deputation; Mr Gaitskell was. Mr Griffiths was in the Chair, but in the course of that discussion Mr Bevan spoke strongly, firmly and even enthusiastically in favour of the proposals, and, therefore, the unity of the Labour Party Executive is, in my observation, real unity and determination to press this matter.

Therefore, while the General Council accept the motion, I repeat that they thought it necessary that some statement should be made, and I hope no one will go away with the idea that there is a wide and growing divergence between us on this subject, because in fact we regard the differences as differences of emphasis, not irreconcilable, and we regard the Labour Party proposals more as an adjunct to a nationalization programme than a substitute for a nationalization programme. (1957 Blackpool Congress Report, pages 460-61.)

When Mr W. L. Heywood concluded the above statement the President, Sir Thomas Williamson, put the composite motion to the vote, and, noting the result, declared it carried, saying 'That seems to be unanimous'.

Although this composite motion, presented to the 1957 Blackpool Congress and carried with such unanimity, once again instructed the TUC leadership to carry out the public ownership mandate of the 1952 Margate Congress, and to honour the pledges solemnly made by the TUC leaders themselves at the 1953 Isle of Man Congress, the speech of Mr W. L. Heywood, on behalf of the General Council, made it clear that the TUC leadership had no intention of doing anything of the sort, but that

Congress had been committed, without either its knowledge or its approval, to an 'investment policy' which was the antithesis of the public ownership policy which Congress had adopted and again and again reaffirmed.

For over five years Congress had been deceived and led up the garden, and even now, by 'double talk', the TUC leadership was keeping up a pretence that it was still engaged on the job of devising a public ownership programme which, in truth, the leadership had discarded.

Note how, in his speech, Mr Heywood claimed that the 'General Council and the Confederation have reached general agreement on a section of the engineering trade, and for that reason we are surprised to see (on the agenda) a motion on the machine tools industry'.

And note his other assurances that the General Council was still devoted to the cause of public ownership. 'At the moment,' he said, 'there are four other documents in the possession of the Confederation . . . The last of them, on the aircraft industry, I make bold to say, as Chairman of the TUC Economic Committee when the document was adopted for communication to the Confederation, is one of the best documents and best examinations of an industry that has ever been turned out in this country.'

He did not reveal what the General Council intended to do with this document, but went on to say that 'a member of the Labour Party Executive, within the last two or three weeks, has expressed the view in the country that a certain section of the engineering industry was soon to be taken into public ownership if a Labour Government was returned'.

Who this member of the Labour Party Executive was who seemed to be determining the policy of the Trades Union Congress Mr Heywood did not say, but he did declare 'I would object if the Labour Party sought to usurp the rights of the Trades Union Congress'!

It is also interesting to note from Mr Heywood's speech that 'representatives of the Labour Party Executive sit monthly with the TUC Economic Committee', although this was the first time for Congress to be told this, nor had the delegates ever been informed, even in the vaguest terms, what subjects had been discussed at these monthly meetings.

Why the secrecy? Was the TUC Economic Committee pro-

H

ducing a public ownership programme or engaged in a con-
spiracy?

But perhaps we were too suspicious, because in a final note did
not Mr Heywood declare, to the accompaniment of approving
nods from his colleagues on the platform, that 'we regard the
Labour Party proposals more as an adjunct to a nationalization
programme than a substitute for a nationalization programme'.

At this stage it was apparent that the policy switch was not
yet completed. The pretence must be kept up a little longer.
Although the 1959 General Election was still two years ahead,
the Congress delegates were anxious to see the promised public
ownership programme which they confidently believed would
enable Labour to win the next election, and without which the
election would be lost.

The TUC leadership realized this, and at that stage it did not
want to create the wrong impression!

Accordingly, when the 1957 Blackpool Congress turned to
consider a motion moved by Mr Jim Mortimer, of the Association
of Engineering and Shipbuilding Draughtsmen, in the following
terms:

That this Congress believes that the greater part of the machine
tool industry should be brought under public ownership,

it was carried without any opposition or qualification from the
TUC leaders, except for a rather intriguing comment from the
President that 'the motion was quite superfluous'. (1957 Black-
pool Congress Report, pages 461-2.)

Events were to show how right he was!

CHAPTER 16

1958 BOURNEMOUTH CONGRESS

THE PRETENCE KEPT UP

Mr W. L. Heywood, Chairman of the TUC Economic Committee, having declared so emphatically on behalf of the leadership at the previous (1957) Blackpool Congress that 'we regard the Labour Party proposals (*Industry and Society*) more as an adjunct to a nationalization programme than a substitute for a nationalization programme', and that 'we should object if the Labour Party Conference sought to usurp the rights of the Trades Union Congress', it was hardly to be expected that but a year later the leadership, at the 1958 Bournemouth Congress, would be so rash as to express a contrary view.

Instead, the leadership continued to keep up the pretence that it was still pursuing the public ownership decision of the 1952 Margate Congress mandate and its own pledges which it made to the 1953 Isle of Man Congress.

Another year was to pass before the TUC leadership completed its policy switch.

In the meantime it was content, in its Report, to inform the delegates attending the 1958 Bournemouth Congress that there had been meetings between the TUC and the Labour Party Study Group, the dates of these meetings and that there had been an exchange of views, without giving even a hint what these views were about. The Report also revealed that the Labour Party in July had published its policy statement *Plan for Progress*, although this statement, like that of *Industry and Society*, had never been presented to or considered by the Trades Union Congress.

Let the Report (pages 301-2) speak for itself:

Control of Industry—Labour Party Study Group

In December a Study Group of the Labour Party National Executive Committee, which was considering the control of industry and related economic issues, asked for a meeting with the General Council's Economic Committee to discuss the scope of the proposed Labour

Party policy statement. The meeting took place on January 23rd and there was an exchange of views on the major issues to be covered.

A further meeting between the Economic Committee and the Study Group was held on May 8th to discuss an outline of the proposed policy statement. A draft of the policy statement was considered by the Economic Committee at its meeting in June, and its views were conveyed to the Study Group. The Labour Party published its policy statement 'Plan for Progress' in July.

Engineering Industries

The General Council have given further consideration to the Confederation of Shipbuilding and Engineering Unions' 'Plan for Engineering', and in March sent a document on mining machinery to the Confederation for their views and as a basis for discussion. The Confederation have promised to let the General Council have their comments on the document as soon as possible.

Aircraft and Machine Tools Industries

A meeting was held between representatives of the Confederation of Shipbuilding and Engineering Unions and the Economic Committee on April 25th to discuss the aircraft and machine tools industries.

It was reported to last year's Congress that there was substantial agreement between the TUC and the Confederation on the need to bring the major part of the machine tools industry under public ownership. It was recognized that an inquiry would be needed to determine the exact extent and method of the takeover, and that this would require further information which only the Government could obtain. There was general agreement that this should be dealt with by the next Labour Government as a matter of urgency, and it was decided that the Labour Party should be informed of the TUC's views, and sent the documents which had been prepared by the TUC and the Confederation.

There was also substantial agreement that there appeared to be a strong case for the extension of public ownership in the aircraft industry, and it was agreed that the TUC document should be sent to the Labour Party with a request for their views.

It will be noted that in the penultimate paragraph an unusual reference appears relating to the machine tools industry, which states that 'it is recognized that an inquiry would be needed to determine the exact extent and method of the takeover, and that this would require further information which only the Government could obtain.'

But why should it have taken six years to reach this conclusion? Since the 1952 Margate Congress, in accordance with the mandate of that Congress, the General Council, its Economic Committee and the TUC research staff had had the public ownership issue under constant examination, yet it took them until the 1958 Bournemouth Congress to conclude that nothing could be done without acquiring 'further information which only the Government could obtain'.

It will be remembered that at the 1953 Isle of Man Congress, in order to get its 'Interim Report on Public Ownership' carried, the TUC leadership declared that it was setting down the policy of the industrial side of the movement and not the political side, and that it was 'laying down right there the historic future of the movement'. Now, five years later, it seems that our historic future depended upon the kind of information which we might be able to extract from the Government, whether it be Labour or Tory!

This, after years of examination and debate, was certainly a new line. But, like Mr Micawber, the TUC leadership is always hoping that something will turn up and relieve them of their obligations to Congress. Did not the publication of *Industry and Society* in July 1957, which was never presented to or considered by Congress, serve just that purpose?

While the delegates never had the opportunity of debating the unusual and unorthodox views set out in *Industry and Society*, its authors had an admittedly difficult, if not impossible, task.

They had to devise a programme that would provide a certain measure of control over an acquisitive, reckless and disorderly system of private enterprise, and which would not conflict with a disorderly trade union movement that, in its present state, was unable to support or sustain a planned economy.

Although they discarded practically every socialist principle in order to accommodate the wishes of the TUC leaders and overcome the effects of the extensive trade union disorder over which they rule, these well-meaning Labour Party draftsmen were to fail dismally in their enterprise.

Instead of achieving the impossible as well as reflecting favourably Arthur Deakin's pronunciamento to the 1953 Labour Party Conference (Labour Party Report 1953, pages 124-5), the product of their literary efforts was, in due time, not only to cost us the 1959 General Election but also to lead to fierce controversies and create unprecedented divisions in our political and trade union movement, as well as to cause countless numbers to lose faith in our fitness to govern the country, and put us in the political wilderness indefinitely.

But let us not anticipate the disasters that then lay ahead. Here, in sunny, sleepy Bournemouth, despite the fact that the TUC leadership had declared its intention to put plans for the public ownership of the machine tools industry into cold storage until 'further information had been obtained from the Government', the delegates attending this 1958 Congress still believed that public ownership plans relating to other industries, particularly those subject to monopoly control, would be pursued. The contents of the TUC leadership's own Report to this 1958 Congress justified that belief.

Of course, in its Report the leadership did make a bald announcement that 'the Labour Party published its policy statement *Plan for Progress* in July', without making any further reference to it, but as that statement, like *Industry and Society*, had never been presented to or considered by Congress, the delegates never anticipated that the mere publication of it would mean that all the public ownership decisions of the previous six Congresses would be wiped out.

In that frame of mind the delegates left the 1958 Bournemouth Congress.

CHAPTER 17

1959 BLACKPOOL CONGRESS

THE POLICY SWITCH COMPLETED

The General Council submitted its usual Report a week or so before Congress opened at Blackpool on September 7, 1959.

What it had to say about public ownership was expressed in section 331 (page 295) in a couple of sentences. Here it is:

Aircraft and Machine Tools Industries

It was reported to the 1958 Congress that the General Council had informed the Labour Party of their views on the future of the aircraft and machine tools industries, on which they substantially agreed with the Confederation of Shipbuilding and Engineering Unions, and that documents had been sent to the Labour Party.

The Labour Party's reply pointed out that their policy statement on 'Industry and Society' committed the next Labour Government to hold official inquiries before decisions on further nationalization were taken. It followed, therefore, that any conclusions they might reach in advance of such inquiries were bound to be tentative and incomplete.

This brief statement meant, although the delegates attending this 1959 Blackpool Congress did not fully realize it, that the strange anti-socialist doctrines contained in *Industry and Society,* which they had never had the opportunity of debating, were soon to be imposed upon them.

The long period of deception, however, had nearly ended. The policy switch was about to be completed.

At the 1957 Congress at Blackpool the Chairman of the TUC Economic Committee had assured the delegates that *Industry and Society* was only 'an adjunct to the Congress programme of nationalization'. Two years later, in 1959, the 'adjunct' no longer held this subordinate relationship to 'the Congress programme of nationalization', because, as a result of the connivance of the TUC leadership and without the knowledge or approval of Congress, the 'nationalization programme' had been scrapped and the 'adjunct', very quietly, put in its place!

Since 1952 successive Congresses, with enthusiasm and a remarkable unanimity, had carried resolution after resolution instructing the TUC leadership to prepare a programme for more nationalization and an extension of public ownership. During this period delegates had devoted countless hours to studying and debating these resolutions which had been submitted to and adopted by these Congresses. It had all been in vain. The decisions recorded were now but scraps of paper.

It was a truly tragic climax, but the TUC leaders who had manoeuvred Congress into this position would now, to their intense satisfaction, no longer be bothered with such things as Congress mandates and 'Interim' and other Reports on this troublesome subject of public ownership.

Thanks to the smart enterprising lads of the Labour Party who concocted *Industry and Society*, the TUC leaders would be able, for many years to come, to deal effectively with any awkward delegates who might raise questions about public ownership in any future Congress.

We cannot but admire the tactical skill of these TUC leaders. They had thrown public ownership overboard; yet, as a result of the patience and care with which they covered their tracks and arranged the necessary alibis, it is difficult to connect them with the crime.

Although these leaders had sacrificed the right of Congress to play its part in shaping our industrial policy, and had voluntarily reduced the status of the trade union movement to that of a poor relation of the Labour Party, they evidently thought these sacrifices, in the circumstances, were worthwhile. After all, *Industry and Society* had saved them, at just the right time, from a very embarrassing situation, and they were relieved and grateful.

If they had been compelled to announce publicly their inability to prepare a public ownership programme because of the outmoded TUC set-up and the competitive and disorderly trade unionism on which it is based, it would have been a disastrous admission which might have imperilled their continued domination.

Now, thanks to *Industry and Society*, the TUC set-up and disorderly trade unionism were not likely to be disturbed, and, inept though these TUC fellows are, they can go on posing as national leaders.

Before the second day of Congress ended, the President interrupted the proceedings to announce that the Prime Minister, Mr Macmillan, had decided to go to the country and had fixed October 8, 1959, as the date of the election. It meant that Congress was committed, although even now few delegates realized it, to an election programme which they had had no part in making.

The following morning the President, with great solemnity, advised Congress that the General Council had decided to invite Mr Gaitskell, the Party Leader, to come to Blackpool to address the delegates and that he had accepted the invitation.

When Mr Gaitskell appeared he had an excellent reception, particularly from the TUC leaders assembled on the platform. During the course of his speech Mr Gaitskell stressed the relationship of the trade unions and the Labour Party, and stated:

You have your industrial job and we have our political job. We do not dictate to one another.

What was in Mr Gaitskell's mind when he made this intriguing statement about not dictating to one another? Was he anticipating the resentment that would arise in the minds of Congress delegates when, later, they read Labour's election programme and found that every important item relating to public ownership which they had discussed and approved for the past six consecutive years had been excluded from it?

While he knew for certain now that he had carried the TUC leaders, and/or the TUC leaders had carried him with them, he had still cause to wonder what would be the reactions of the cheering, unsuspecting delegates and millions of other trade unionists when they realized the policy trick that had been played upon them. During the coming election campaign could these supporters of public ownership be expected to canvass and support policies alien to their convictions, which, as delegates to the Trades Union Congress, they had never debated, because the TUC leadership had denied them that opportunity?

Mr Gaitskell was quite right when he declared that 'we do not dictate to one another'. Of course there is no dictation, because invariably the Labour Party does what the TUC leadership wishes it to do!

It is true that the TUC leaders were not the authors of *Industry and Society*; they were only its silent and powerful backers, as the record shows. If these leaders had not been completely out of sympathy with the mandates of Congress, proposals for the extension of public ownership would never have been excluded, as they were, from Labour's 1959 election programme. The revisionists would never have been able to commit the Labour movement to such anti-socialist policies and place it in such a helpless position without the ready acquiescence of the TUC leaders. And this they did in defiance of the decisions of their own Congress.

How completely the TUC leaders switched Congress policy was shown almost immediately after the 1959 Blackpool Congress, when the Labour Party published for the consideration of the election its 1959 General Election programme, *Britain Belongs To You.*

On the subject of nationalization this is what *Britain Belongs To You* declared:

WE HAVE NO OTHER PLANS FOR FURTHER NATIONALIZ-ATION. BUT WHERE AN INDUSTRY IS SHOWN, AFTER THOROUGH ENQUIRY, TO BE FAILING THE NATION WE RE-SERVE THE RIGHT TO TAKE ALL OR ANY PART OF IT INTO PUBLIC OWNERSHIP IF THIS IS NECESSARY. WE SHALL ALSO ENSURE THAT THE COMMUNITY ENJOYS SOME OF THE PROFITS AND CAPITAL GAINS NOW GOING TO PRIVATE INDUSTRY BY ARRANGING FOR THE PURCHASE OF SHARES BY PUBLIC INVESTMENT AGENCIES SUCH AS THE SUPER-ANNUATION FUND TRUSTEES.

Compare this declaration and try to reconcile it with the Margate Congress decision of 1952. Compare it with the pledges made by the TUC leadership when it presented its own Interim Report on Public Ownership to the 1953 Isle of Man Congress. Compare it with the decisions of Congress in the following years and with the speech made by the Chairman of the TUC Economic Committee to the Blackpool Congress in 1957, which is reproduced on pages 109-112, and we are content to leave the reader to form his own conclusions.

It was now clear to all that the TUC leaders had welshed on their 1952 mandate and broken their 1953 pledges and the decisions of subsequent Congresses.

A heavy price had to be paid for their inexcusable conduct.

Part, but only part, of the price was paid by Mr Gaitskell himself on the very day of the General Election when, hours before the count had been completed, he conceded a decisive victory to the Tories.

After Labour's defeat some of the prominent supporters of *Industry and Society* (which the late Mr Arthur Deakin seemed to have inspired by his threat to take his Union away from the Labour Party) proposed that the name of the Labour Party be changed. It must be admitted that, in the circumstances, that was quite a logical suggestion! Perhaps these revisionists thought that by doing so they could catch up with the 3,000,000 trade unionists who, according to Harold Hutchinson of the *Daily Herald,* had deserted Labour and lined up with the Tories on the fateful election day October 8, 1959.

CHAPTER 18

THE BIG SIX

The TUC as at present constituted can never be fully representative of the trade union movement, nor can it ever reflect the enormous wealth of talent, most of which now lies dormant, in this movement.

The TUC is democratic in appearance only. Even Tory Cabinet Ministers must, periodically, submit themselves to the will of the people. The TUC 'Cabinet' leaders have a better arrangement: they have devised a scheme which relieves them of the inconvenience of being subject to the will of the membership.

Later we will show how this remarkable scheme works. Here we refer to the lopsided character of the movement as depicted by the scales on the opposite page. It shows that, according to the figures submitted to the 1959 Blackpool Congress, there are 186 Unions affiliated to the TUC, but that six of them are so big that their total membership exceeds that of the remaining 180.

This means that provided the 'Big Six' act in unison, as they usually do, they can push the trade union movement in whatever direction they want it to go. It also makes certain that, irrespective of judgment or ability, those who control both the TUC and its officers shall always be drawn from within the Big Six or from those who are both loyal and subservient to their rule.

On issues of policy, or on important or even unimportant appointments, however, there is never a clear line between the Big Six and the rest. There are varied reasons for this. Some of the smaller Unions like to demonstrate that they are on the side of the big fellows for the advantages it gives, while other small Unions may be motivated by loftier considerations.

While these movements to and fro on the part of the small Unions may confuse the mind and blur the view of the onlooker, the Big Six are undoubtedly *the* arbiter of TUC policy. The Big

Six may, for some reason or other, lose a round or two, but, as the record shows, they never lose the contest.

The Big Six, aided by some of the smaller fry who for various reasons choose to line up with them, can determine who shall hold almost every office within the trade union and the Labour political movement. They can decide the composition of Congress Standing Orders Committee, delegations at home and abroad, and who shall sit as trade union representatives on Government Boards, Committees and Inquiries, as well as select who shall speak on trade union subjects on radio or television.

It is understandable that the leaders of any movement or party must always protect the interests of the movement or party in every conceivable way. But the Big Six, or the so-called leadership of the TUC, do not, in fact, represent the interests of a movement, nor are they elected by the movement; they only represent the interests of this powerful group.

Anyone who does not subscribe to the views and policies of this group, no matter how able he may be, has no opportunity to play his part in the movement.

What opportunities there are are reserved for the mediocre, the yes-men and the sycophants.

The effect of the Big Six rule is as disastrous to the movement as are the consequences arising from sustained inbreeding on the part of members of a tribe or dynasty.

The Big Six are content to repeat the slogans of yesterday, but beyond this the survival of their rule transcends all other considerations, and if it is thought that any new idea or any new policy (such as a national wages policy or the extension of public ownership or trade union reform) does not ensure that survival, it is either decisively smothered or sidetracked.

A national wages policy and the extension of public ownership are both essential for the establishment of a properly planned, democratic and prosperous industrial economy. But these are unattainable while we have a lopsided, unplanned, disorderly trade union system, upon which the Big Six thrive. This, and not the feeble efforts of the leaders of private enterprise and Tory politicians, is the greatest obstacle to the realization of our trade union aims.

But the cleverness of the TUC leadership, dominated by the Big Six, must be acknowledged. They never give the slightest indication that they do not favour public ownership. They avoid committing this tactical blunder, but by skilful manoeuvre, as the earlier chapters of this book have shown, they commit Congress, without Congress being aware of it, to an 'investment policy' and other anti-socialist doctrines set out in *Industry and Society*, which are the very antithesis of public ownership. To keep up a democratic appearance it took this leadership several years to complete this difficult operation. But patience enabled it to achieve its reactionary purpose.

A pseudo-democratic appearance is also maintained by the annual selection of the TUC President on a seniority basis. What could be fairer than that? It gives the impression that in the TUC hierarchy the representatives of the 180 small affiliated Unions have equal opportunity with the representatives of the big Unions. But the fact remains that the representatives of the smaller Unions are selected with great care, and if there is the slightest doubt about their loyalty to the set-up they have no hope of ever having the chance to establish a seniority claim.

The TUC President is not selected by Congress. The representative of the small Union only achieves this office if he is chosen by the big fellows to be a member of the General Council and commands their continued approval until he can pass the seniority test. But he must be careful what he says and does, otherwise he'll never reach it.

FRANK COUSINS

It may be said that our criticism of the Big Six does not hold water in so far as Mr Frank Cousins, the present leader of the T & GWU, does not follow in the Bevin and Deakin tradition but takes his own independent line, whether it pleases his other 'Big' colleagues or not.

We regard Mr Cousins as a man of great promise. It is true that he has antagonized his TUC colleagues by his opposition to wage restraint and the H-bomb. These colleagues, from time to time, have said very nasty things about him and have even voted against him in favour of lesser men when he has submitted himself for certain offices.

But in the light of these minor incidents it would be presumptuous to say that he intends, now or in the future, to depart from the Bevin and Deakin tradition and pursue a more progressive and intelligent line, which is so urgently needed.

Frank Cousins is in a difficult position. He is a powerful leader because he commands a vote of one and a quarter million members, but it must be remembered that these members are not concentrated in one or two spheres but are spread over 200-250 very dispersed industries with no common ties except those of being members of the T & GWU.

If these one and a quarter million members were contained in fewer industries, closely associated with each other, Frank Cousins' power would be enormously increased and would provide him with great opportunities, which are now denied him, to use his undoubted talents.

He is an avowed socialist, but until he realizes that socialism, even in its most rudimentary form, cannot possibly be achieved by and through the general type of trade union he now leads, he will make little impact on the future development of the trade union movement and will be little more than a nuisance value to his TUC colleagues.

He must realize, from his own bitter experience, how chaotic the trade union movement has become and how frequently it violates the very principles it was created to promote.

In one industry after another large numbers of T & GWU members having no dispute with their employers are thrown idle and deprived of wages as a result of some other Union, without any consultation with the T & GWU, deciding, officially or unofficially, to down tools.

The London bus strike was a classic example of trade union disorder. For six long weeks in 1958 T & GWU busmen fought an epic struggle inflicting great hardship upon themselves and their families. The Government, the London Transport Executive and the press were all arrayed against them—and so was the National Union of Railwaymen, whose leaders instructed their members, who run the trains in the Tube below London, to continue at work and blackleg the members of the T & GWU who normally drive the buses on the streets above.

This was an example of trade union solidarity which Frank Cousins is not likely to forget. It shows, as did the amazing conduct of the leaders of the competing Unions in the more recent dispute in the railway industry proper, the price the workers have to pay for running our Unions on the principles of private enterprise.

How is Frank Cousins likely to react to these and other happenings that have taken place in the short time since he was elected to the post of General Secretary of the T & GWU? Will he become reconciled to the leadership of his powerful TUC colleagues and pursue a line in accord with the tradition of his predecessors, and preserve a set-up which is becoming more decadent every day that passes?

Or will he be content to pursue his own independent line while still disregarding the urgent need to re-cast the TUC machinery?

If he follows the first course the TUC leadership will be delighted; if he continues the second line, while ignoring the need for trade union reconstruction, he will just inconvenience the big fellows and that's about all. The leadership will simply re-align their forces to offset the loss of his votes and continue to pursue their disastrous policies, and Frank Cousins, like A. J. Cook once was, will be just another *enfant terrible*.

The trade union movement is in dire straits, from which, under the present TUC management, it cannot extricate itself. It seems certain that as time passes the movement's plight will become even worse: industrial relations will become more and more chaotic; trade union control over both employers and its own members will get progressively weaker, and as three million trade unions deserted Labour in the 1959 election it may well be that some of the affiliated Unions, despairing of ever being able to reform the TUC set-up, will sever their relations with it.

This is a situation that a Tory Government will welcome. It will provide the justification to bring trade unions under legal control, depriving them of much of the freedom they now enjoy.

Frank Cousins and a few other progressive but rather silent members within the TUC must realize this disastrous state of affairs which the TUC leadership has created.

There is no health in the movement, and it will remain so until the basis upon which leadership rests is radically changed and the number of Unions, now totalling 186, substantially reduced (say to thirty or forty) and related to clearly defined industrial boundaries, within which any competitive trade union activity would be prohibited.

1

Such a trade union structure would end the rule of the Big Six. Thirty or forty Unions, roughly comparable in size, designed to serve all the workers' interests in a rationally defined sphere, would enable the workers within such sphere to participate effectively in joint consultation and also play their proper part in management, both of which are now impossible.

Leadership elected on this basis of thirty or forty Unions would be representative of the entire movement and not of a privileged section, as is now the case, and it would enable the wealth of talent that now lies dormant in the movement to be utilized to the benefit of all.

Elections to offices in the trade union movement and in the Labour Party would reflect the wishes of the membership, and not the prejudices of a couple of big fellows. Trade Union Executives would have real functions to perform and the means to provide educational facilities for their members and research facilities for themselves.

This scheme, or anything like it, would, however, be strenuously opposed by the TUC leadership. For the past twenty-five years they have resisted every suggested change. They are not likely to give way now. But would the millions of trade union members who are victims of the present trade union disorder oppose it? They should be given the opportunity to decide.

CHAPTER 19

THE BLACKPOOL INQUEST

At the Special Conference of the Labour Party at Blackpool on November 28 and 29, 1959, Mr Gaitskell and many other speakers gave varied reasons for Labour's third consecutive election defeat on October 8, 1959.

How decisive that defeat was, and how Labour's political power has declined, is shown below by the number of Labour Members returned in each of the General Elections since 1945.

General Election 1945 — 393 Labour Members returned
        ,,   ,,   1950 — 315   ,,   ,,   ,,
        ,,   ,,   1951 — 295   ,,   ,,   ,,
        ,,   ,,   1955 — 277   ,,   ,,   ,,
        ,,   ,,   1959 — 258   ,,   ,,   ,,

What is the cause of this depressing trend in Labour's fortunes? Surely it cannot be entirely attributed to Tory propaganda, Mr Hurry and the Institute of Directors? Nor can it be said that the decline stems from the fact that Labour's own TV stars were less competent than those of the Tories, or that the Tory leaders displayed superior electioneering skill.

Nor did the electors—including three million trade unionists —desert us because we had neglected to revise our 'out of date' standing orders, nor because we had failed to re-name the Labour Party.

We failed because Labour sought to represent itself as something that it is not, and many of Labour's supporters intensely disliked the fraudulent disguise. Labour's proclaimed preparedness not to displace capitalism but to share the brass with it was, to them, like entering into a partnership with Satan, which proved successful in driving far more worshippers from Labour's church than it brought strangers in.

Instead of keeping faith with Labour's fundamental philosophy and basing our political programme on that philosophy, enlightening and converting the electors and elevating their moral and social standards, our political leaders presented them with a hotch-potch of left-overs from capitalist jumble sales, dressed up with Liberal co-partnership trimmings.

But what's done is done. Can Labour, after seeing its Parliamentary ranks decline from 393 Members in one election to 258 in another, take steps to arrest this downward slide and recover from it?

Without looking into the crystal ball it is plain to see that unless Labour drops its strange and disastrous doctrines and is re-converted to an extensive public ownership programme, and effective steps are taken to ensure its complete and satisfactory implementation (which is only possible by the elimination of the present trade union disorder and the almost medieval structure that now rests on it), Labour's decline will continue until it is of little political consequence.

At the Special Blackpool Labour Party Conference, which was a mass inquest on the 1959 election, Mr Gaitskell described many factors which, he thought, had contributed to the defeat. Perhaps it was discretion on his part not to mention the mismanagement of their affairs by the TUC leadership, which constituted the greatest deterrent of all to Labour's victory. Perhaps, if he had been so minded, he would also have revealed that even *Industry and Society*, which he had sponsored and which had so dismally failed, was only designed to offset the effects of this mismanagement of the TUC in respect of industrial affairs.

But must a great trade union and Labour movement decline and disintegrate because a small clique of leaders are out of touch with the world in which they live? Under their domination there seems, in any case, no alternative to Tory rule—unless something even worse arises.

Hitherto, trade union aims and ideals influenced an ever-increasing number of progressive-minded electors, and also commanded ever-growing support from the workers themselves.

These trends have now been reversed. Disgusted by the absence of any semblance of statesmanship from trade union leadership, and by its complete failure to end the internecine war between Union and Union, in which both workers and members of the public are victims, these progressive-minded electors, having no desire to vote Tory, are now, in increasing numbers, either declining to use their votes or turning to the Liberals.

That's the result of TUC leadership, which claims to represent over 8,000,000 members.

It has no moral or intellectual guidance to offer its own members or the electors, either when times are normal or in periods of crisis. When problems arise affecting the interests and welfare of its own people, the TUC leadership believes it best to ignore them. It proceeds in the belief that if it does nothing it cannot be blamed for doing it!

If the leaders of one Union are endeavouring to cut the throats of the leaders of another, and, by strike action, doing irreparable harm to the cause of trade unionism in the process, it is not the affair of the TUC leadership. The leadership is content to leave it to the forces of attrition or the leaders of the Church or Tory arbitrators to bring about a truce or a settlement. It would be difficult for Mr Gaitskell to claim that this sort of conduct helped him in Labour's election campaign!

He did say, however, that 'in the past the pendulum has always swung against the Party in power after one, or at most, two periods of office', and went on to say that in the last few years the pendulum had ceased to swing. In one of the most important points of his speech Mr Gaitskell dealt with the 'changing character of the labour force', and revealed that 'now there are fewer miners, more engineers; fewer farm workers and more shop assistants, fewer manual workers, more clerical workers; fewer railwaymen, more research workers; and the typical worker of the future is more likely to be a skilled man in a white overall, watching dials in a new modern factory'.

'It is the inevitable result of technological advance' in the new industrial revolution. But Mr Gaitskell was unable to point to or applaud any constructive work on the part of the TUC leadership in blending the new with the old, and ensuring the allegiance of the worker in the white overalls as well as the worker in the moleskin trousers.

The TUC leadership has neglected and ignored the important problems arising in this transitory period. In its journey through the new world it is content to depend on Bridlington principles and the good old demarcation lines!

It lacks vision even when its own interest is at stake.

Later, Mr Gaitskell bluntly declared that 'public ownership and nationalization lost votes'. As public ownership, or nationalization, was a forbidden topic in Labour's election campaign and we gave the Tories every opportunity to misrepresent it, we can't deny that, in the circumstances, we lost votes. But we regret that Mr Gaitskell refrained from telling his audience how the TUC leadership helped to discredit public ownership and nationalization in the public mind, and that there is now little hope of retrieving its popularity, or Labour's fortunes, while the TUC household remains in its present disorderly state.

But why did Mr Gaitskell strive so hard to revise the famous Clause 4? It is only an adornment to the Constitution anyhow! The TUC leadership will never allow it to be implemented, so why should he worry? The TUC leaders silently share his views, so if, as a result of rank and file pressure on this issue, he throws in the towel, it will not upset his leadership.

This accord, however, between himself and the TUC leadership is not likely to bring him any nearer the Premiership. Indeed, as we see it, if the present TUC set-up continues, Mr Gaitskell's only hope of fame is to occupy the post of leader of the Opposition longer than any previous occupant. Because, strange as it may seem, in the present circumstances Labour cannot win an election without the TUC and it cannot win one with the TUC.

It must be a depressing thought to Mr Gaitskell that his future is so bleak. He must realize that public ownership is imprinted on the minds and the hearts of Congress delegates and countless others, as the many conferences of the affiliated Unions held during the early part of 1960 have shown. If he pushes public ownership farther into the background he may strengthen his ties with the TUC leadership, but only by increasing the disharmony in this already riven and troubled movement.

Can Mr Gaitskell overcome this dilemma? He is an intelligent politician; in the hope of containing the mounting pressure from Union delegates for public ownership he may, as a price of his own survival, try to come to terms with it by offering to add a few other industries to his very restricted 'take-over list'. But he would need to proceed very carefully.

He has, of course, history and his own experiences to guide him. The ascendancy of George Lansbury and his sudden departure from the leadership; the appointment of Clement Attlee and his leisurely retirement; and the tussles that preceded his own election to the leadership must have made him aware how decisive is the role of a few trade union leaders in rejecting the candidates they dislike and getting elected the one they prefer.

The lot of the leader is a hard and difficult one. Unless he walks in step with this small group of TUC leaders and fashions his policies in accord with their private wishes he will not only imperil the block votes they control but will also risk losing the support of many of their sponsored candidates in the Parliamentary Party.

If he fails to walk in step with these few big fellows of the TUC he may also lose the cheers and support of the professional politicians who, regardless of occupational qualifications and demarcation niceties, make a point of taking out membership cards with those Unions which count most in power politics.

Mr Francis Williams (Clement Attlee's Public Relations Officer) wrote in Forward on December 25, 1959, that Herbert Morrison had no cause to bleat about Attlee staying in office long after he should have retired in order to keep Morrison out. Mr Williams claimed that he had a ringside seat and saw what went on. That may be so.

But how leaders (and Party Treasurers) are chosen and the circumstances in which they quit are not usually seen from the ringside. To have that privilege one would require to watch the principal promoters through the keyholes of private hotel suites and certain Millbank offices in order to ascertain how the leader is selected and how long he is to lead. His subsequent election, secured by the required number of block votes in the open forum, is but a democratic formality.

But let us not be too pure. In a lopsided, disorderly movement in which it is impossible to carry out democratic practices, this peculiar technique of leader selection is unavoidable.

Whether Mr Gaitskell, however, can reconcile the wishes of Congress delegates and rank and file members for the extension of public ownership with those of the TUC leadership who want to prevent this extension, we do not know. But we certainly do not wish that his leadership, or its duration, should be dependent upon a small trades union clique, powerful though it be, which is far from being representative of the trade union movement and has already brought incalculable harm on that movement.

In his Blackpool Conference peroration Mr Gaitskell declared:

Our defeat must not be a depressive or a sedative, but a challenge to keep up the spirit of attack again and again and again, until we win.

But unless he attacks the right target it is most improbable that he will ever win.

CHAPTER 20

CAN TUC LEADERSHIP CHANGE
OR BE CHANGED?

We believe that the present TUC set-up is an anachronism in the modern world and that its leaders can only preserve it by subordinating progressive policies to anti-social ones.

It is also our conviction that under its present domination Britain has no socialist future, and that neither the trade union movement nor the Labour Party will ever be able to realize even its most moderate aims.

The present TUC establishment and those who preside over it are the product of many decades, and, year after year, like an imperial household, it strives to consolidate and strengthen its position in relation to those subject to its rule; and this always presents the danger that the preservation of its rule becomes more important than the interests of its subjects.

Over the years, under TUC leadership, the trade union movement, instead of becoming a planned, orderly movement, has become a fragmented and disorderly one, incapable of any effective collective action. This fact and the remarkable constitutional powers it possesses means that the TUC leadership can pursue any course it wishes without serious challenge. It can successfully withstand any attack and resist any wind that bloweth. It is secure in its Congress House citadel.

If any member of the leadership (the General Council) retires or dies or is publicly disgraced, there will be no difficulty in filling the vacancy with the right type upon whom the leadership can safely rely.

Whatever the leadership does inside the Council always commands the necessary support outside the Council—thanks to the way the members of the Council, with the acquiescence of their respective Executives but without the knowledge of their rank and file members, use their block votes.

137

Perhaps it is not unreasonable to fill casual vacancies in this way. But surely in the annual election of the TUC leadership the vote of the rank and file does count? Unfortunately, in the present TUC set-up it doesn't.

The miners, year after year, voted unanimously that Mr Arthur Horner, their General Secretary, should occupy a seat on the General Council, but the block votes of leaders of other Unions who know little or nothing about the mining industry kept him off. But to disregard the wishes of nearly 700,000 miners in this way shows with what skill the TUC ballots are conducted. Nothing is left to chance. The exclusion of the crusader or the critic or anyone likely to disturb the serenity of the General Council is of the utmost importance!

To ensure this, the thirty-five places on the Council, according to a rule long out of date, are allocated to industrial groups. But that is not all. Some twenty of these places are presented to certain Unions as free places, without any form of election!

The number of places secured on the TUC General Council in this way in respect of the 1959 'election' are shown below:

GROUPS IN WHICH NO BALLOT WAS HELD

Elected without ballot	Union	No. of members
	Group 2 — Railwaymen (3 seats)	
Greene, S.	National Union of Railwaymen	355,440
Hallworth, A.	ASLE & F	65,438
Webber, W.	Transport Salaried Staffs' Association	87,322
	Group 3 — Transport (other than Railways) (3 seats)	
Cousins, F.	Transport & General Workers Union	1,224,588
Forden, L.		
Yates, Sir T.	National Union of Seamen	62,500
	Group 4 — Shipbuilding (1 seat)	
Hill, E.	United Society of Boilermakers, Shipbuilders & Structural Workers	94,649
	Group 6 — Iron and Steel and Minor Metals (2 seats)	
Douglass, H.	Iron & Steel Trades Confederation	107,471
O'Hagan, J.	National Union of Blastfurnacemen, Ore Miners, Coke Workers & Kindred Trades	22,403
	Group 8 — Printing and Paper (1 seat)	
Willis, R.	London Typographical Society	20,007

Group 9 — Cotton (2 seats)

Roberts, Sir A.	National Association of Card, Blowing & Ring Room Operatives	45,024
Wright, L.	Amalgamated Weavers' Association	61,166

Group 10 — Textiles (other than Cotton) (1 seat)

Sharp, L.	National Union of Dyers, Bleachers & Textile Workers	61,787

Group 11 — Clothing (1 seat)

Newton, J.	National Union of Tailors & Garment Workers	115,718

Group 12 — Leather, Boot and Shoe (1 seat)

Robinson, S.	National Union of Boot & Shoe Operatives	77,245

Group 14 — Agriculture (1 seat)

Collison, H.	National Union of Agricultural Workers	135,000

Group 16 — Civil Servants (2 seats)

Houghton, D.	Inland Revenue Staff Federation	37,971
Smith, R.	Union of Post Office Workers	165,487

Group 18 — General Workers (3 seats)

Cooper, J.
Hayday, F.
Williamson,
    Sir T.
	National Union of General & Municipal
	    Workers
		774,940

3,514,156

Thus, out of the thirty-five members of the General Council, twenty-one were declared elected without any contest at all. Twenty-one places had, in fact, been reserved for them. Is this arrangement democratic? Of course it isn't. Can it be successfully challenged? Not likely! There are powerful vested interests unwilling to relinquish privileges which may have been justified years ago but are not now.

But that is not all. These Unions shown in the table, that have been allocated twenty-one uncontested places on the General Council, represent block votes amounting to 3,514,156, which they have no need to use in respect of themselves but which, instead, they use to elect the remaining fourteen members!

If this is not a case of 'backing it both ways', it is an effective way of retaining the commanding heights of control.

It is unlikely that the TUC leadership will ever voluntarily abdicate from its privileged position, and in the light of the voting procedure of Congress there is no hope of bringing about any radical reform through that body.

The TUC leadership alone has the power to alter its character or change its direction, and it has no inclination to do either. Only when some unusual combination of progressive forces emerges, able to push aside this TUC rump, will the trade union movement be able to practise democratic principles and advance on its historic path.

Sidney Webb, G. D. H. Cole and other notable historians, who devoted a lifetime to the study of the evolution of the trade unions, expressed in their writings many warnings about the evils that would arise if the Unions were allowed to go on developing without any form of control, but they never succeeded in persuading the TUC to make a thorough examination of this development with a view to exercising control over it.

Now, as a consequence, although we are the oldest trade union movement in the world, we are one of the most disorderly and undisciplined. That is not only our view; it is also the view of some notable TUC leaders.

For instance, Mr C. J. Geddes (now Sir Charles), who introduced the 'Interim Report on Public Ownership' at the 1953 Isle of Man Congress, speaking at Taunton some three years later, declared:

What I cannot understand is, if the trade union movement and its spokesmen demand a controlled economy, whether they believe that you can succeed by having a trade union movement which is, after all, at present like a series of guerrilla groups in a jungle. (*The Times*, March 7, 1957.)

Whether Sir Charles was either commended or reproved by his TUC colleagues for making this realistic statement we do not know, but there was no follow-up.

A little later, while addressing the Professional Workers' Conference in London, Sir Tom O'Brien, ex-President of the TUC, expressed the view that trade union affairs were not what they should be.

The trade union movement, he said, would be well advised to make an objective assessment of its structure and organization, including industrial and negotiating machinery in all fields of activity, rather than to have improvements thrust upon it by the Government and commissions. (*Manchester Guardian*, April 29, 1957.)

We have no means of knowing what the reactions of Sir Tom's TUC colleagues were to his plea for an 'objective assessment of trade union structure and organization'. We recall, however, that at the 1955 Southport Congress, when a plea was made for a similar objective assessment of trade union organization in the nationalized industries, Sir Tom, speaking on behalf of the TUC General Council, then advised Congress to reject it!

Yet another ex-President of the TUC has also expressed doubts about our trade union health. Sir Alfred Roberts, addressing the Bolton Trades Council, declared that:

the trade union movement has grown up without planning and controls, and he expressed doubt as to whether the structure of the trade unions is in line with present needs . . .

There is some ground for talking about a merging of forces with other Unions which are pretty well in the same class of industry, but he did not want to see big General Unions. He didn't think that would be a desirable development at all, and in fact he thought there may be a case for reducing the size of the big Unions. (*Daily Herald*, October 31, 1957.)

That three very influential TUC Knights should, in their different ways, admit that the trade union movement is out of joint, led the hopeful to believe that the 'wind of change' was at long last beginning to blow through the corridors of Congress House. Alas! it did not prove to be even a zephyr. Whether or not these three Knights were reprimanded by their TUC colleagues for seeking to disturb trade union disorder, nothing further has been heard from them. As the TUC leadership is representative of competing interests and conflicting organizations, which makes it impossible for it to reach common agreement on general policy, wage policy, organization policy or anything else, it would have been surprising if we had heard anything more about it!

Mr Alan Birch, General Secretary of the Shop Assistants' Union, has also pleaded, without any success, for TUC reform.

The individual members of the TUC leadership are themselves victims of their own set-up and, by the nature of things, they are incapable of reforming it. The only hope is that progressive trade union forces will come together and bring about its complete reconstruction.

CHAPTER 21

SHOP STEWARDS

A POTENTIAL FORCE FOR GOOD

Without the services of shop stewards our present rickety, disorderly and competitive trade union structure would soon collapse, and although they are frequently abused and maligned it is within their power, if they care to exercise it, to rid the trade union movement of these disorderly and competitive attributes that are now slowly but surely destroying its influence and rendering it incapable of carrying out its declared purpose.

The necessary reform cannot be brought about through the normal channels of the Trades Union Congress, nor by means of the efforts of any single affiliated Union. We believe, however, that the shop stewards, acting collectively, could achieve it. Success could not be denied to a shop stewards' movement dedicated, as a beginning, to the single and simple task of eliminating every semblance of trade union conflict and the establishment of complete trade union unity in every workshop and factory, without regard to stupid, out-of-date boundaries that now divide and weaken the workers.

It is to be hoped that such a movement will arise and succeed in arresting the decline of this great trade union movement.

But who and what are shop stewards? B. C. Roberts, in his excellent book *Trade Union Government and Administration in Great Britain*, has helped us to answer this question. On page 69 he has given a good description of a shop steward's duties:

(1) He is concerned with recruitment to the Union and stimulation of Union organization and membership. (2) He is responsible for seeing that members pay their contributions regularly, and many undertake the job of collecting and paying them over to the branch secretary. (3) He is charged with the task of ensuring the carrying out of existing agreements, working practices, customs and habits within a shop. (4) He has the duty of representing the members' interests, and of negotiating on their behalf, in any matters of difficulty or dispute which may arise, with the foreman or management.

Of course, not every shop steward in every trade or industry carries out all these duties. In some trades and industries, where there are no competing Unions, the performance of these duties is simple and straightforward and presents little difficulty to either the stewards or the Union. In the mining industry, where there is only one Union, there are no stewards as such. Those who act on behalf of the miners are known as Union or lodge representatives and are subject to the rules of the Miners' Union and the direct control of the Miners' Executive.

There are a few other trades and industries controlled by a single Union where collecting stewards and sick stewards operate, but these, like the lodge representatives in the mining industry, function exclusively for the Union in control of the trade or industry concerned.

But marked differences arise in the functions of shop stewards in an industry where there are several competing Unions operating. The lot of these shop stewards is an unenviable one. The individual shop steward is expected to further the interests of the Union to which he belongs and, at the same time, co-operate with other shop stewards who may belong to ten, twenty or thirty and more other competing Unions. His loyalties are frequently strained. He may wish to go contrary to the instructions of his own Union and fall in line with the wishes of his fellow workmates attached to several other Unions. He is a victim of trade union disorder but he and his fellow shop stewards do what they can to control it, for which service they get little credit. Indeed, they are subject to constant attack from almost every quarter, yet if they were to cease functioning for a few days the entire process of production would grind to a standstill.

It is one of the strange features of our industrial life that while shop stewards in an industry controlled by one Union are regarded as inestimable fellows, the shop stewards in an industry where there are many competing Unions, and resultant disorder, are looked upon as disrupters and saboteurs. It is no less strange that some of the leaders of the bigger Unions, who are mainly responsible for this disorder and benefit most from the services of the shop stewards, make the most frequent and vicious attacks upon them, which gives many outsiders the impression that they are something the devil himself has created.

Almost every strike and industrial upset is invariably attributed to the shop stewards, and should there be no stoppage or incident that can be used to denigrate them some of the TUC leaders can always be depended upon to convey sensational stories to the press, based on information from undisclosed sources, alleging that groups of shop stewards are in the pay of foreign powers and are planning to stop all essential export industries and also to upset our entire national life.

The late Mr Arthur Deakin achieved fame as a revealer of secret shop stewards' plots. He was very good at this. Periodically he would release to the newspapers the most fantastic accounts of the intentions of the conspirators and the plots they were supposed to be hatching.

When these plots did not materialize that meant that the country had been saved by Arthur's timely warnings!

The feelings of the shop stewards never seem to matter much. No doubt they feel aggrieved and resentful that publicity seeking trade union leaders should make such serious, unsubstantiated charges against them and trail the good name of the shop stewards in the mud.

Since Arthur's death several of the TUC leaders have tried to emulate him by repeating his old hair-raising scares. In Arthur's former role the leaders of the NUG & MW and the AEU, to mention but two groups, have tried particularly hard to make our flesh creep, but so far they have put up a pretty poor show. They don't frighten the old ladies half as much as Arthur did!

The leadership that brought nationalization into disrepute adds further discredit to itself by blackening the good name of the shop stewards, who are the victims of the trade union disorder which they had no part in creating.

But the fact that members of the TUC leadership go on making these silly attacks on the shop stewards through the medium of the press shows how nervous and unsure of themselves they are. These are the actions of leaders who have ceased to lead and hope, no doubt, that by publishing these frequent scares they will alert MI.5 and all the forces of the law to stand by and protect them!

If these leaders are not abusing or vilifying the shop stewards to cover up their own failures and incapacities, why don't they take steps to abolish shop stewards?

Let them try it out by withdrawing their own shop stewards

from, say, London Airport, where there are seventeen trade unions, and from Briggs, where there are twenty-two trade unions. Let these leaders transfer the functions of the withdrawn shop stewards to the full-time officials of these Unions and see the naked effects of what trade union disorder can be like without shop stewards to control it.

But after dispensing with the services of the shop stewards what a pantomime there would be if, in these two undertakings where there are thirty-nine different Unions, thirty-nine different lots of full-time officials moved in to take over their duties. There is little place for trust and mutual help among competing Union Executives. In the absence of 'shop steward convenors' which Executive would be trusted by the other Executives to call meetings of the workers? That might prove insuperable, and perhaps, in order to prevent one Executive from having an advantage over the others they might all agree for the management to act as 'convenor' on their behalf!

Having disposed, in some fashion, of the problem of who shall act as convenor, how will these thirty-nine Executives deal with the numerous disputes arising on the shop floor? Would the thirty-nine lots of trade union officers stand by ready to march on the management immediately a dispute is reported, or would disputes and deputations be regarded as the private affair of the Union with which the disputed worker was in membership?

If, in undertakings where competing Unions operate, these Unions dispensed with the services of the shop stewards, the present disorder would soon become complete chaos, and the very leaders who now criticize the shop stewards most violently would be squealing the loudest and begging them to resume their shop stewarding duties without delay, because inter-Union squabbles, membership plundering and privilege hunting, without the restraint of the shop stewards, would quickly reach unprecedented proportions.

These are not the only evils of competitive trade unionism. Some Unions are employing a new tactic of entering into secret talks with certain employers for the purpose of making 'deals' that will ensure, at a price, favoured treatment for these Unions at the expense of other Unions and their members.

A trade union movement that ceases to serve a common purpose and is so muddled and at war with itself will continue to decline in influence and membership strength. It is unlikely that new entrants to industry, familiar with the use of the slide rule, precision tools, time and motion study and the processes of planned and ordered production, will become enthusiastic supporters of an inefficient, wasteful and second-rate trade union machine.

The lamentable state of the trade union movement was really shown by the appointment of Mr Alfred Robens, M.P., as Labour Relations Adviser to the Atomic Power Constructions Ltd. in connection with their projected nuclear power station at Trawsfynod, which would employ some thousands of men and take four or five years to complete. His job would be to deal with disputes and 'ensure that the site is a happy one for all'. Although recent events have prevented Mr Robens from taking on this job, the fact that the Company offered it to him and that he accepted it seems to show that both Mr Robens and the Company feared that if numerous competing Unions organized on the usual demarcation lines it would turn the site into something resembling the Tower of Babel, and that without a 'ringmaster' or a 'super shop steward' the Unions would be unable to control the labour force or adequately represent it.

In the light of this admission it may be said: Why have Unions at all?

Mr George Woodcock, Assistant General Secretary of the TUC, writing in *Forward* on October 23, 1959, declared that 'there is a hardening in the attitude of the non-union half of the population against the trade unions', and 'the attitude of the general public towards the trade unions has also become less sympathetic'. That is serious enough, but when trade unionists themselves begin to lose confidence in their own movement and, in large numbers, cease to be inspired by it, a far graver situation presents itself.

There may be many reasons for this but the chief reason is the dismal failure of the TUC leadership to guide and direct the trade union movement and its amazing refusal to deal with the problems that beset it. And the trade union movement is paying the price of its negligence.

Sir Vincent resigned for health reasons from the TUC General Secretaryship on September 9, 1960, on which date he was succeeded by Mr George Woodcock.

INDEX

THE END